Pra
LEAVING FAITH,

MW00573122

"Through her breathtakingly honest account of her early life in rural Australia enduring the brutal hypocrisies of her family's religious beliefs, Lynne Renoir shares her path to empowerment, discovering her connection to the divine within. Brilliantly written and inspirational!"

— DR MANJIR SAMANTA-LAUGHTON MBBS, Dip Bio-energy, author of *Punk Science and The Genius Groove*

"I wish it had not taken Lynne Renoir so many decades to tell her profoundly moving and inspirational story, but thank goodness she found the courage to write it. Renoir's journey from the suffocating and sometimes dangerous religious environment of her childhood to the spiritual playground of the psychosphere is the adventurer's journey. Renoir's is an extraordinary tale, and she, a woman charged with a unique fearlessness to believe."

— CARMEL NILAND, author of *Our Spiritual DNA: The Ascended Masters* and *The Evidence for Our Divine Ancestry*

"*Leaving Faith, Finding Meaning* paints a vividly poignant picture of life growing up in a religiously controlled and often abusive family environment in mid-20th-century Australia.

It's filled with compelling stories that illustrate how the weight of her father's religious fervor shaped the first half of Renoir's life. From stamping on her ambition to be a teacher and dismissing her spirited nature and incisive intelligence as aggression to the final beating that led her to flee her home and family, Renoir evokes both outrage and empathy with her honesty and courage.

Renoir's journey from religious indoctrination to spiritual freedom is a beautifully written and inspiring story for anyone seeking to find their own pathway to liberation."

— SANDIE SEDGBEER, TV/Radio host of What is Going Om and founder of The No BS Spiritual Book Club. www.sedgbeer.com

"There is always a plan and in these pages you will read about a most difficult journey, but nonetheless, a journey with great purpose. Within Lynne's core was a seed of passion to know and be one with God, but each time she tried to nurture that seed in her younger years, the castigating situation at home would snuff out the light needed for it to grow. Despite the odds stacked against her, each struggle, each seeming disappointment, and each experience unfolded one petal at a time to reveal the full beauty of Lynne's true purpose and spiritual abilities. This true story is a triumph of the human spirit and the remarkable way we are guided by unseen hands, even when that guidance is difficult to see."

— NANCY J MYERS, Speaker, Medium, Orb Photographer, Host of "The Spheres of Spirit" Podcast, and author of *Entering the Light Fantastic: Discovering Life after Life Through Orbs* and *Encircled by The Light Fantastic: A Deeper Journey into the Light with Orbs*. www.theorbconnection.com

"*Leaving Faith, Finding Freedom* is a courageous story. Lynne Renoir engages the reader from the outset. She is a curious and thoughtful child whose spirit is stifled by the religious environment she is raised in and by the abuse she suffers at the hands of her father. Renoir's early life astounds. The stories of her adulthood will astonish. Renoir describes her communication with the spirit world and long-dead philosophers — which opens up her psychic abilities. Readers will find this beautifully written memoir inspiring — ultimately, Renoir's is a journey to spiritual freedom."

— GAIL TORR, www.galaxymediamanagement.com

What early readers are saying about
LEAVING FAITH, FINDING MEANING

"I was pulled right into Lynne's life from the first page of this book. It reads like a great novel, and, like a great novel, has a surprising plot twist. But, of course, this is not fiction, and I am in full admiration of this lady."

— E. HARRIS

"So gripping, I felt I went on her journey with her."

— FRANCES M.

"A fascinating story! Lynne's research on the abuse of men gave me a whole new understanding of the violence that men can also suffer, and told me more about how she was able to put her own experiences at the hands of men aside to try and help men who have had the same experiences as her."

— GEMMA HANSEN

"This book starts like an autobiography and also reads deliciously like great fiction."

— ELLEN WOOD

Leaving Faith, Finding Meaning

A Preacher's Daughter's Search for God

Lynne Renoir

Lynne Renoir
PUBLISHING

ISBN 978-0-6483043-6-4

Cover and interior design by Damian Keenan

Published by

Lynne Renoir
PUBLISHING

CONTENTS

Introduction

I grew up in a deeply religious family whose every thought and action were dictated by the need for approval from a punitive God. In my home, to displease God was evil. And to disobey my father, who saw himself as God's representative in the family, was a heinous sin.

I am not alone in this situation.

For most of human history, the word "God" has been understood as a love that is beyond description. Yet in various countries throughout the world, thousands of people have been cruelly treated because of their involvement in a particular religious tradition.

Like many such people, my life has been a story of struggle. I was forever trying to discover what would give my life meaning. For the first twenty-three years, I was physically abused by my father, who proclaimed the teaching of God from the pulpit. He held firmly to the view that every word in the Bible had been dictated by God. And he was attracted to the words of Solomon that he must use "the rod" to discipline his child. Beatings began at a young age and ended when I eventually found the courage to leave home, never to return.

Being raised in this kind of home caused much conflict within me. Was my father really doing the will of God in using the cane whenever I forgot something or had an accident? It was not as though I ever did anything terribly wrong. I was never even tempted to get into any kind of trouble throughout my teenage years. But I had to be totally submissive to whatever my father decreed. And I was not allowed to challenge anything he said. My obedient and dutiful mother supported everything my father did, and never once tried to protect me from his excesses.

The above problems would have been bad enough, but in trying to engage with the Christian faith, I was confronted with the fact that I did not measure up to the qualities the Bible lists as an outcome of belief. I had none of them. It never occurred to me that the reason for my predicament was the treatment I was receiving. The scriptures did not make allowances for abusive fathers.

A further problem was that many people who held beliefs similar to mine exhibited the required qualities. But what really complicated the matter was that these qualities could often be found in people who held different beliefs, and in those who had none.

I had so many questions and no one to answer them. I wondered whether there could be a fundamental difference between consciously held beliefs and a deeper part of our being that may be involved in the process of transformation. Pursuing this question led me to undertake postgraduate studies in Psychology and Philosophy. Quantum theory also fascinated me. I wanted to know more about the nature and behavior of matter and energy, and I read everything I could on the subject.

As a result of my extensive studies, I was eventually freed from the idea that I was a failure, and that there is a God who sits in judgment on me. I discovered instead that everything in the universe is one. This meant that there could be no supreme being who is beyond all that we know, and who constantly evaluates our behavior. This was not an overnight discovery, nor did it occur in a flash of inspiration. Rather it was a lifetime journey that I wish to share and to help anyone else who is seeking to understand the meaning of our existence.

This book is the story of my journey to freedom.

Prologue

"It's a girl." It couldn't be! Only sons were a sign of blessing in the Bible. Was this a judgment from God?

The baby's father, a Church official, said evil entered the world through Eve, and women have been the downfall of men ever since.

He strides up the steps of the maternity ward. "God's curse on Eve," he muses, "pain in childbirth. The women in this ward should not be given pain-killers. And they should be subject to their husbands in all things." His own wife, at least, understood that.

Bed after bed he passes, looking into the condemned eyes. From the far corner of the ward his wife sees the look that had terrified her for the ten months of their marriage. It does not change as he catches her eye. She crunches her shoulders. This must have been her fault. He was close to perfect and God should have rewarded him. He bends over and kisses her with cold lips.

"Well, I'm pleased it's healthy." The sound is forced and flat. "I suppose you're all right?"

His wife does not answer. They had both been so sure it would be a boy. "R" for Rodney had been embroidered in blue on the tiny clothes. How could a girl wear them now?

Baby is brought to mother. She raises the little face to the harsh eyes.

"She looks like you," a timid voice suggests. He glances briefly, then moves towards the window.

"I've got to finish my sermon. I'd better be off."

Baby is confused by the noise and bright lights. She longs for closeness again. Mother gives her the breast and she is content. But soon, unfamiliar hands take her away.

Home from hospital. Mother places the bassinet on her side of the bed. Father tosses and turns.

"What's that snuffling sound?"

"Is she disturbing you?"

"I can't sleep with that noise. You'll have to put her in the back room."

"I think she should stay with me, just for a few weeks."

"No!"

Baby is taken away. She hears the door close. She cries, but no one hears. She wakes in the night and cries again. Silence. She is alone.

"I can hear baby," Mother says next day. "I'll go and see to her."

"Don't."

"But surely I could just hold her."

"Is she due for a feed?"

"No."

"Then leave her alone."

No one comes. Baby is frightened. The silence is endless. Life in the womb was so good. She dreams of warmth and nourishment, and she is back there. She dreams again. Such a good baby. Always asleep.

But then she wakes, and the vision goes. Loneliness overwhelms her. Eventually Mother comes. Baby clings to the breast and won't let go.

At the clinic they said Mother was doing a great job. Baby had put on weight.

Home to the crib. Again the door closes. Baby can't bear it. She tries to think. She can't understand the pain, but the process creates an energy within her. It saves her life.

The struggle to be born had become the struggle to survive. The universe was hostile. The fight had begun.

CHAPTER 1

Early Days

God punishes those who fall below his standard of perfection. During my early years I did not question this idea. Punishment—both by God and my father—was gradually forming my identity. But I struggled to understand what I could have done to deserve the treatment I was receiving, and whether there was any hope of escape.

The time was the early 1940s at the height of the Second World War and the place was a modest home on the outskirts of Brisbane. Our dwelling sat on a steep slope, low at the front and with high piers at the back. Like those of our neighbors, our small front yard was bare of shrubs or trees. The back yard, beyond which was bushland, descended in four terraces. The bottom one was all weeds—long sharp blades that cut your fingers and thick fluffy undergrowth. Holes in the weathered grey palings of the back fence allowed a free flow of wildlife. Snakes dozed on our side, unaware of passing from public to private property. One slid up under the house and curled itself around a leg of the green gas copper, narrowly escaping Mother's attack with a broom. Mother could handle anything, but when I thought of that horrible creature close enough to strike at her, I realized how much I wanted to protect her.

In the garden near our parents' bedroom, feral cats mated. Father roared at them, hosed them, threw stones at them but they defied him. In retribution he drowned all their kittens. I thought it was cruel, but he said they didn't feel anything.

The outhouse containing the lavatory stood at the end of the top terrace. We were too far from civilization to have sewerage, and too poor to afford a septic tank. The small timber structure provided strange acoustics when my younger sister, Deborah, stood on the seat and sang through the triangular gap formed by the inverted V-shaped roof.

The only feature of the narrow, sloping terrace below the outhouse was the incinerator, a three-sided stack of blackened bricks. Mother was known throughout the neighborhood for her regular burn-offs, though her fires were lit only after she had assured herself that no one within smoke range was planning to hang washing. Mother never kept anything for more than a few weeks. Cards, letters, even photos of unidentified people, fell indiscriminately into the flames, together with advertising junk and butchers' wrapping paper.

Between the incinerator and the weeds was a terrace containing vegetable gardens, a strip of level ground on which we played a gentle version of cricket, and the chook pen, made of wire netting strung between wobbly square poles. Bits of tin and corrugated iron formed the walls and roof of a shelter, adjacent to the side fence. In the open area the roosters fought and the hens roamed free, except when pinned to the ground to satisfy the bodily needs of their masters. I felt sorry for the hens as they struggled to free themselves, but I never questioned the right of the roosters to overpower them. That was the way God had ordered things.

Inside the shelter were two boxes lined with straw—miniature versions of the manger of Bethlehem—and perches of parallel bars half way between the ground and the roof. Near the entrance was a round silver tin for shell-grit and a china bowl filled with water.

Other food—sodden bread scraps and wheat grains, was thrown over the fence. We were supposed to scatter it evenly, but invariably it fell in piles, giving yet another opportunity for the males to demonstrate their lordship of the pen.

Scrawny white Leghorns and corpulent black Orpingtons dwarfed the scurrying brown Bantams, whose maternal instincts drove them to sit on eggs too large to have been produced by their tiny bodies. Each morning I squelched my way through the slosh and gently extended my arm into a nest, pulling it out quickly when a sharp beak dug into my skin. Normally hens did not object to the removal of their eggs, but they sometimes resented being deprived of time to deliberate upon their readiness for motherhood.

A few days before Christmas each year, one of the senior hens whose eggs had provided the foundation for sponge cakes, flummeries and lemon meringue pies, was grabbed by Father and taken to a chopping block. Deborah and I hid in the bedroom when we saw him take the axe. Did the hen struggle? Did she feel pain? I did not want to know the answers, but we could not avoid the sight of the bird a few hours later, dripping with blood, hung upside down by her feet from a clothes line under the house.

Whenever we had a surplus of eggs, we shared them with the Thompsons, who lived across the road. They lent us their goat, but a snake killed him. "He was old anyway," they said, trying to hide their pain. Most of our neighbors cared for each other in practical ways. Washing would be removed if the owners were out and a storm was approaching. Other people's gardens were watered during holiday periods and their animals were fed.

The fences in our street, mostly low brick or wire on timber frames, allowed clear views of the homes and gardens. Saturday mornings saw exchanges of male opinions from front lawns, between stints of gardening, on topics from house painting to politics. Father loved any kind of audience, waving his grass clippers when making a point or slicing the air with his hands, clippers cast aside.

The Cartwright-Brownes, who owned both a brewery and a two-storey mansion, lived next to the Thompsons. Their brick fence looked down upon the surroundings, its imperious height signifying the disdain of its owners for the common people around its borders. Dense trees, which prevented the curious from gaining too much information, provided just the narrowest glimpses of upper frills on lace curtains. We never saw the Cartwright-Brownes, only their ghostly shapes through the darkened windows of their limousine as it slid silently out from its hiding place in the shadows. Even the gardener seemed invisible, other than when his capped head bobbed up for a moment above the level of the fence.

Our immediate neighbor was Mrs. Ryan, a stooped, wrinkled lady with a mournful smile who gave us lemons from her tree. We visited her place only once. Thick black curtains, which were never opened, fell almost to the floor. In the darkness we saw strange whitish figures gleaming along a polished mantelpiece. Mother explained later that these were the figures of saints. Each day Mrs. Ryan walked a mile to the Catholic church with the help of a stick. To me, she was even more devoted to God than our parents were, but Mother said Catholics offered prayers to saints and that this was wrong.

In our district everyone knew everyone else's business. The disappearance of a teenage girl "for about eight months" was discussed by all the women other than the girl's unfortunate mother, whose supervisory negligence was universally condemned. Mothers with sons and no daughters must have felt safe in their superiority. The failings of their offspring were known to very few.

One woman in a tiny cottage was shunned by all. "She's a de facto," I heard Mother whisper. I wanted to ask what that meant, but the look on Mother's face ensured my silence. Had the lady committed a crime? She seemed so nice.

The weekday bus into the city was filled with women discussing breastfeeding, children's illnesses and problems at the local school. But one subject was never raised. It was only alluded to in laughter at male foibles—a safety valve, I was to discover, when the pain became too great. "Women are better people than men," was all Mother said.

If Mother's belief had been right, my gender should have given me an advantage. But I was soon to learn that in the eyes of God and my parents, the only acceptable way for a woman to behave was to be meek, quiet, and submissive.

CHAPTER 2

Going to School

Each morning I reached down to the end of the bed where my only doll, Lucy, was lying face up. I pressed her little shape tightly to my chest. It didn't matter that one arm was coming off from the shoulder and the white stuffing was falling out. She seemed to know how unhappy I was when Father punished me—most of the time because he didn't like what I said. It was hard for me not to cry as he smashed his large hands across the side of my head.

My fifth birthday came and went. We did not have parties.

"Put those toys away, Lynne," said Mother one evening as she heard Father coming up the back stairs. She didn't mind how much mess we made when he wasn't around, but any room he entered must not show any signs of children's fun. I was about to clear the toys when I remembered I had left Lucy underneath the house. I brought her upstairs and was putting her to bed when Father came in.

"You haven't done what your mother asked."

"I was just going to," I said defiantly.

"Don't you answer back!" he shouted, pushing me onto the bed. He rolled me over and smacked me hard—this time on the bottom.

I could not understand why Father was always so angry with me. The things I was doing wrong seemed so unimportant. I thought about the night his mother came to visit. I had gone to bed at the usual time, relieved that Father's attention was directed to someone else. But the next morning his face had a black expression that terrified me.

"I was ashamed of you," he said. "You left the room without saying goodnight to your grandmother."

"I just forgot," I said, in a tone of suppressed irritation.

Had I begun, at an early age, to imitate Mother, I could probably have avoided punishment by pleading for his forgiveness whenever I upset him. But though I wanted to be like Mother, I was not prepared to beg Father for mercy. That would have been an admission that his punishments were just. He hit me across the head. "Maybe that'll help you to remember next time." There were so many things I had to remember. Life was full of traps. I was always tense, always on guard.

"You mustn't be late for your first day at school," said Mother, opening the blinds the next morning. "I think the rain has gone, but remember, don't cross the creek if the water is over the bridge." She lifted up the mosquito net and gave me a glass of orange juice. Her face was gentle and kind, but something wasn't right. She was never happy when she looked at me. I wondered if she, too, thought I was bad.

Mother had made me a blue and white cotton check dress with a sash tied at the back and a bag made of the same material to hold my school cleaning sponge. It was on a long piece of tape, threaded through the top of the bag, that went around my shoulder. My school bag felt like stiff cardboard, and I practiced opening and closing the metal clips and threading my arms through the straps. One of my shoulder blades stuck out and rubbed against the bag. Inside was my lunch of Vegemite sandwiches, a piece of cake with pink colored icing, and a mandarin.

I had to walk a mile to the school. There were no buses and Father would not allow me to own a bike. After breakfast, I said goodbye to Deborah and tried to cuddle Mother, but she pushed me away.

"Don't speak to strangers," she warned, "and don't accept a lift from any man you don't know."

I waved at the front gate and tried to look strong, but I was frightened at having to walk such a long way alone. The furthest I had ever been by myself was to the store down the street. On the way to school I saw groups of girls who all seemed to know each other. I thought I would be the only person with no one to talk to.

On entering the school grounds, I heard squealing and laughing. It was such a contrast to the quiet of home. Children were playing on slippery slides and see-saws. Never again would I go on anything like that. A few months earlier, Deborah and I had been for a ride on a merry-go-round. She giggled the whole time, but I gripped the horse's head and closed my eyes, desperately hoping the music would stop so I could get off.

At the top of the steps in the kindergarten building was a lady dressed in black. She looked older than my grandmother, with a mouth that curled down almost to her chin. Her black and grey hair straggled around her face like a dirty floor mop. I wondered if she had ever smiled in her whole life.

"Stand in straight lines here," she said in a deep voice. Two other ladies helped us get into line. I hoped I would get one of them as my teacher, but as we marched up the steps, I found myself in the same room as the lady in black.

"My name is Miss Hertzog," she said when we were all seated. She picked up a polished stick.

"You see this? I use it to hit any child who is naughty." A girl in front of me started to cry, then a boy, then it seemed everyone was crying. I could have cried, too, but decided I would be braver and stronger than everyone else in the room.

It was an awful place. The walls were a dirty yellow. There were no pictures, no toys, just rows and rows of desks covered with deep scratch marks. Attached to the front of each desk was a seat which folded up on a hinge. On top of the desk was a slot which held a black slate. Miss Hertzog showed us how to pull the slate out. Grey-colored sticks, "slate pencils," sat in a groove parallel to the slot. The sponges for cleaning the slates had to be brought to school each day and placed on a shelf under the desk.

I was sitting next to a boy with thick glasses. I had never been close to a boy before, and thought he had a funny smell. I tried breathing through my mouth, but then it got too dry, so I turned my head away. We practiced drawing letters as Miss Hertzog walked up and down the aisles. I heard her footsteps behind me.

"Stop!" she said to the boy next to me, as she hit him on the left hand. "Use your other hand." The boy tried several times without success, and threw his slate pencil back in the groove.

"Keep trying!" said Miss Hertzog, banging her stick in front of him on the desk. My own hands started to shake.

School was so much like home. Children were treated like the enemy. Did parents and teachers think we were dangerous—like the Japanese? What harm could we do? We could not move from our seats and we were too frightened to make any sound other than crying. At home I could at least argue back, even if it resulted in a beating. In the classroom I felt like a prisoner.

At the end of the lesson Miss Hertzog pointed to the door. "You can go downstairs and return in twenty minutes when you hear the bell."

I followed the other children downstairs to the school canteen where flavored milk was being served in aluminum mugs.

"Strawberry or chocolate?" asked a pleasant lady behind the counter.

"Strawberry, please," I said, never having seen flavored milk before. I loved the strawberries Father grew, but the sweetened pink milk had a strange taste. As the bell rang, I didn't know which was worse—being on the school ground with children I was too frightened to talk to, or sitting in class looking at the cruel teacher.

At lunchtime some of the children went to the shop across the road and bought pies and soft drinks. In our family we were not allowed to have things like that. I sat under the school in the semi-darkness and ate my lunch, looking out on the other children playing. They all seem to have friends, or at least had no problem in making them. They were enjoying their freedom while I was in a cage. I was alone, and I was different.

I wondered if that was why I was always being hit. Being different meant being bad. Mother and Father believed God was not happy with me, and were trying to make me good. I wanted to be good too, to have friends, and be like other children. But there must have been something inside me that would not let that happen.

CHAPTER 3

God Loves Boys

"Face, hands, feet, teeth, toilet?" The familiar question came from the kitchen.

"Yes Mummy," we responded as we raced to the bedroom and jumped into Deborah's bed. Mother came in carrying our favorite book, "Stories from the Bible." She sat at the end of the bed and pulled out the bookmark with its shiny gold tassel.

"Tonight's story," she began, "is about a lady called Hannah. Her husband loved her very much, but she was unhappy because she had no children. She prayed to God, 'Please give me a son.' She kept asking, year after year, but nothing happened."

It seemed to me that parents always wanted sons. I wondered if that was why all the important people in the Bible were male. God and Jesus too. We didn't know any boys, except those at school, but we never spoke to them. Mostly they were rough and noisy, particularly the ones from the boys' home, and they hit each other. Deborah and I never did things like that.

"Then one day," Mother continued, "Hannah was in the temple, crying. She said to God, 'If you give me a son, I will give him back to you. He will serve you all his life.' God heard Hannah's prayer and gave her a son. She called him 'Samuel.' Hannah kept her promise and she took her little son to the temple. He grew up there with the priest, Eli." I knew the story well, and I began thinking about Samuel in my class at school. He was special too—a quiet Jewish boy with lovely big brown eyes.

"One night," Mother read on, "he was lying in bed and he heard a voice in the dark calling his name. He rushed to Eli, and said, 'Here I am. You called me.' But the priest said, 'I didn't call you. Go back to bed.' The voice called Samuel's name again, and once more it was not Eli. The third time it happened, Eli knew it must have been God who had spoken. He said to Samuel, 'This time when you hear the voice, say "Speak Lord, for your servant is listening."' The voice came again, and Samuel spoke to God as Eli had told him to. Then God gave Samuel an important message."

At the end of the story we knelt down beside the bed, our hands pressed over our eyes. Mother knelt beside us.

"Dear Heavenly Father," she began. We repeated the phrase.

"Thank you for giving us such a happy day." Again the phrase was repeated, until the end of the prayer. We kissed Mother goodnight and climbed into bed. The light went out and I lay in the darkness, wondering what it would be like to hear God calling my name.

"Dear God," I prayed, "I'm only a girl but please speak to me. I am listening." I repeated the prayer three times. I waited... and waited. Thoughts about Jesus came into my mind. I remembered some things he had said to people when he was on earth, though I couldn't think of any words he'd actually spoken to a child. I thought of things God might say, and tried to imagine that he was actually talking to me, but in the end, I knew I had made it all up. *God is not interested in me*, I thought.

It rained heavily overnight, forming puddles on the worn patches in the middle of our long back stairway. Between the piers that supported the outside walls of the house were rows of vertical battens. Sunlight shining through the battens created stripes on the white sheets hanging on the line underneath the house. Thick cross beams stretched diagonally from the ground to the top of the piers. Deborah, who had no fear of heights, was climbing up one of them.

"Look at me!" she called out. I watched in fear and admiration as she crawled higher and higher. On reaching the top she put her hand on the metal plate resting on the pier, signifying the accomplishment of her mission

"It's easy," she said, crawling down backwards. "You have a go."

Not wishing to be outdone, I put my hands and knees on the beam and slowly moved upwards. Halfway along, I looked down at the dirt. My body froze. The ground was six feet below me. I pictured myself lying there helpless, an ambulance man coming with a stretcher to get me. I tried to edge backward but found I could not move.

"I've got to get down. Help me!"

"I'll get Daddy," said Deborah.

"No, don't. I've got to make myself do it." I closed my eyes and screwed up my face. Then, gripping the beam firmly with both hands, I slowly forced my left leg backward, then my right leg. One at a time, I loosened my grip with each hand and moved them down the beam. Stopping after each movement, I continued until I felt the toes of one foot touching the ground.

"I'm never going up there again!" I said angrily.

At the side of the water tank, a short distance away, I had made a special place for myself where I kept a small blackboard on an easel. The story of Samuel, which Mother had read the night before, was the story of a hymn I loved. I opened the book and began to copy it onto the blackboard.

Hushed was the evening hymn,
The temple courts were dark,
The lamp was burning dim

31

Before the sacred ark;
When suddenly a Voice divine
Rang through the silence of the shrine.

It concluded with a prayer that, like Samuel, we would be obedient to God in life and death. I wanted to do what the hymn said, but what did that mean for me?

"The Bible says children should obey their parents" Father would often say. But supposing parents made mistakes, or disobeyed God, what were children supposed to do then? Could children pray to God by themselves, or did you have to be a very good person before God would hear you? Perhaps I was so bad that God could not answer my prayer the previous night.

I finished writing out all the verses and then said them to myself over and over again. Then I walked outside on to the grass, where I couldn't see the board, and recited them right through without a mistake. It seemed that the only time Father ever liked me was when I had done something clever, so I ran upstairs with the hymn book to show him.

"I can recite all the verses of 'Hushed was the evening hymn'," I said. Father looked up from his morning paper.

"All right," he said. "I'll hear you."

I handed him the book. At the end of the recitation he smiled. "That was perfect," he said. I was excited. I had made him happy.

The next day at lunch Father was sitting in his usual position at the head of the table. I was glad I never had to sit next to him.

"Lynne, you've forgotten to use your serviette." I pulled a face as I placed the forgotten article on my lap. Learning table manners was boring—like arithmetic at school.

"How did it go this morning?" Mother always asked the same question when Father was preaching at another church.

"There was a good response. And it's always very humbling when people express such enthusiasm and appreciation."

I was confused. Father was never humble, but he was always having humbling experiences.

"This was a new sermon," he said.

Oh no, I thought, *not another one.*

"Now for the introduction," he began, "I told them a story about..." I realized, too late, that I had forgotten to ask someone to pass the salt. Father could not bear it when his speeches were interrupted by trivial comments about items on the table. I gave Deborah a nudge, but she must have been too frightened to respond. I then leaned across the table, and my arm was just long enough to reach the salt-shaker. But as I pulled it back towards me, my elbow knocked Deborah's glass, spilling water onto the table cloth. Father stopped in the middle of a sentence, lifted himself a few inches off his chair, and reaching over the table, banged the side of my face and head with all his might. It really hurt, and I felt dizzy. I said nothing but glared at Father, enraged.

"I'll give you another clip over the ear if you're not careful."

I turned my head away from him and tightened my fists under the table. He continued with his sermon. There was no other sound in the room. Knives and forks were lifted and lowered in silence.

After some time I began to eat, and having no interest in the wisdom Father had imparted to his morning congregation, I wondered whether, as a child, he had ever made mistakes or had accidents. Of course, the answer had to be 'yes.' *Then how dare he demand a standard from me that no child could ever reach? How dare he!* It seemed to me that he was somehow taking the role of God in the family—that he had been given divine wisdom to know what punishments would be appropriate for his rebellious daughter.

CHAPTER 4

Accidents are Forbidden

It was Sunday, my favorite day. I put on my new white dress so I could wear it to Sunday School. As I walked down the street, the morning had that relaxed feeling—people reading the papers on front verandas or taking a leisurely stroll before the sun rose too high. The annuals were in full bloom, and I could still smell the freshly-cut grass from Saturday's mowing.

I was carrying three eggs in a basket, which I had collected from the hens that morning.

"Be careful not to drop them," Mother had said. "Remember, they go to poor people."

I loved everything about Sunday School: the smiling superintendent, the beautiful young teachers—so different from the ugly Miss Hertzog at school with her stick—and the music! Miss Dawn's long white fingers made the piano sing. Although our family could not yet afford a piano, I hoped that my small hands would play for God one day.

The previous week in story time, the teacher had taught us about love. She reminded us of the song, "Jesus loves the little children, all the children of the world." She pointed to a picture on the wall showing Jesus surrounded by children from every race, his hands on their heads. "God loves us too," the teacher had said. "He is our heavenly Father."

I was puzzled about love. I often asked Mother, "Do you love me?"

Her answer was always the same, "All mothers love their children."
I desperately wanted her to say, "Yes, I do love you," but the answer
never came. Her reply seemed to mean that although we all loved each
other because we happened to be in the same family, Mother could
not love me for the person I was. Perhaps she was disappointed that
I was nothing like her. But surely that was not my fault. I believed
Jesus loved me, but I wasn't sure about God the Father. Was he like
my own father—always looking for opportunities to punish me? "The
fear of the Lord," Father would say, "is the beginning of wisdom. We
must never offend God by breaking his laws." I was certainly afraid
of Father, but was I supposed to be afraid of God as well?

Mr. Thompson, the neighbor who had lent us the goat, was
driving up the hill in his old Whippet. Deborah and I used to count
the number of times he had to turn the crank handle before the car
would start each morning. Apart from the windscreen, it had no
windows. The driver's door had fallen off, and Mr. Thompson had
not bothered to replace it. He had two children, and I would watch
in wonder as his eyes lit up whenever he spoke about them. He gave
me a big wave, his arm unrestricted by any portion of the car, as he
directed it around the potholes in the unsealed road. Recent storms
had gouged out deep channels, and there was little left of the original
level surface. I waved back to Mr. Thompson as I continued walking,
but my foot caught the edge of a pothole. My body was flung forward
in one terrifying moment and I landed sprawled out on the road. The
basket had fallen from my hand, my new dress was splattered with
mud, and something was wrong with my leg.

Slowly I sat up and saw a deep, jagged cut on my left knee. It was
stinging—it really hurt. I cried but did not call out. Wiping my eyes
with the back of my arm, I leant over to pick up the basket.

"Oh no! The eggs—they're broken."

With blood pouring from my leg, I limped back up the hill to the house, tearful and afraid. I knew Father would say I had sinned, but perhaps God was punishing me as well.

"What on earth have you done to yourself?" asked Mother, looking down at my injured leg.

Hearing the noise, Father came striding along the hallway scowling. His thin lips tightened, his body stiffened, and he stared— not at my injured leg, but at the eggs dripping from the basket.

"Get in there!" he yelled, his long finger pointing to his bedroom.

"But her leg is cut," said Mother. "It'll bleed all over the floor."

"I'll attend to that later," he snapped.

To me, my parents' bedroom was the only beautiful room in the house. Fine lace curtains and delicate soft green wallpaper gave me a feeling of peace. I loved the dressing table, adorned with Mother's crystal. The large mirror was in three sections, with a wing on either side. The beveled edges created brilliant rainbow colors. I could place the wings at various angles to make my reflection longer or wider, and at certain angles I could see my face a hundred times. Alone in this magic room, I could forget that it had become a place of pain.

Father was wearing the black trousers of his Sunday suit and a singlet. He had not finished dressing. A few days earlier he had gone into the bush to look for a tree branch from which he could make a cane. He had apparently decided that he was not following the Bible closely enough in smacking me as hard as he could with his bare hands. "Fathers," he had said, "were told they must not 'spare the rod.'"

I wanted to say how sorry I was about the eggs, but it would not have helped. I was not allowed to have accidents. The sound of the door closing behind me filled me with terror.

"Three valuable eggs wasted—all because you were too lazy to watch where you were walking." I listened in silence. He went over to the cupboard, pulled out the cane, and waved it a few times in the air. How I hated that swishing sound.

"Pull your pants down," he snarled. I obeyed, bent over, and buried my face in the sheets. It was not only that my body was exposed. To my father, on those occasions, I was less than human. In my presence, he would say to people, "Lynne's like a wild horse. And it's my job to break her in."

I waited for the first stroke, biting my lip. It came suddenly. I winced at the pain, this time on my thighs. Then I felt the cane touching me lightly, higher up. Then another stroke of pain. Father breathed heavily but said nothing. How many more? The cane touched me again, marking the place where it lashed me the third time. I bit into the sheet, but I would not make a sound. I knew that my refusal to scream and beg for mercy infuriated Father. He regarded it as willful pride and punished me even more. But I remained silent. He could force me to submit my flesh, but he could not control my mind.

"Get dressed," he said in a different voice—though it contained no hint of remorse. It was more like exhaustion. Again I obeyed.

"I'll fix that leg now," he said flatly. What did he care if I was in pain? Roughly he washed away the blood. "Keep still," he snapped as he bandaged the leg. "Well, I hope you've learned your lesson. Now go."

I went out to see Mother, wanting her to put her arms around me, or at least ask me how I was. She just looked at me as if nothing had happened. It was not as though I expected her to criticize Father in front of me. Over the years, I came to wonder why she never once tried to protect me. Whenever I was in disgrace with Father, she seemed to reject me too.

I followed Mother and Father to church later that morning with bandaged leg, aching buttocks, an old dress, and no eggs. Father, and probably Mother as well, must have believed I had let God down. But could the Creator really expect perfection from a child? I was confused about that. Deborah walked beside me. She had seen what had happened but was powerless to help me. My only consolation was that I hadn't cried. I hadn't given in to the man whose authority I was forbidden to challenge. I resolved on that day that whatever he did to me, I would fight him with everything in my being.

CHAPTER 5

Forgetfulness must
be Punished

"Lynne, I can't find your red cardigan," said Mother, holding an armful of clothes for the washing. "Did you bring it home with you yesterday?"

I could not remember. Part of my mind was never where it was supposed to be. I was not interested in ordinary, everyday things—only the big questions that had no answer. Why did Christians thank God for life? I was angry that I had not been given a choice about my existence. I would not have opted for life unless I could have chosen my parents—a mother who could really love me and a father who would correct me without being cruel.

"I must have left it at school," I said, "but I can't think where."

"This is getting beyond a joke," was the exasperated response. "I'm going to tell your father."

I deeply resented the occasions that Mother made such threats and carried them out. Why couldn't she deal with me herself? At least that way, the punishment would have matched the seriousness of the offense. But with Father, it depended on his mood, and Mother must have known how brutal his treatments could be. I went into my bedroom and waited. Each day I promised myself I would try not to lose things. But my overcharged mind refused to be confined. What cruelty would Father think up for me this time? I heard his footsteps in the hallway.

"You're coming with me," he said coldly. "Put your shoes on." I obeyed. He grabbed me by the shoulder and pushed me out the front door and down the steps. "We're going to the school." I took a deep breath and hurried to keep up with Father's long strides as we walked the rest of the way in silence.

It was Saturday morning. The neighbors were working in their gardens and friendly greetings were exchanged. I felt betrayed by all the people who liked Father. He could be so charming outside the home. By contrast, I was not regarded as particularly "nice." I said what I thought, and that was unacceptable behavior in a ten-year-old girl.

As we turned the corner at the end of the street, I looked anxiously towards the house of Mrs. Lamont, the local gossip, who could usually be seen leaning her heavy body on one of her side fences. After exhausting her immediate neighbors, she would engage the woman on the other side of the road, the sound of her rasping voice being interrupted only by that of an occasional passing car. A few weeks earlier, I had been to the corner store. It was owned by Mr. Dickson, a scrawny man with a bony face. He had never married and treated children with contempt.

"That will be eight shillings," he said, as he handed me the groceries. I gave him a pound note—or so I believed. He gave me two shillings change.

"Well, why are you standing there?" he asked.

"I'm waiting for the rest of my change," I replied.

"You gave me ten shillings," he insisted.

"No, it was a pound. Look in the cash register and you'll see it."

He opened the register and pulled out a ten-shilling note.

"This is yours," he said, waving it in the air.

"You're trying to trick me," I said.

"You are a little spitfire, aren't you?"

I was enraged. "Don't you call me names!"

Despite my bravado, I was terrified of adults. A few of them were more kindly disposed to me than my parents were, but generally, I had become suspicious and distrustful with older people. My anger towards them arose because I knew that, as a child, I would always lose in any conflict with them, no matter how just my cause.

Realizing that I had lost again, I strode out of the shop and raced back home to tell Mother what had happened. She then relayed it to Father. Showing no interest in whether or not I had given Mr. Dickson a pound note, he demanded to know who else was in the store.

"Mrs. Davidson and Mrs. Lamont," I replied.

Had Father contacted Mrs. Davidson, I knew she would have been on my side. A professional woman, she had said to me, "People may not understand you at times, but you are a special person." Of course, Mother and Father rejected Mrs. Davidson's assessment of their daughter. It was a strange experience for me to have an older person who believed in me. I was tired of hearing Mother discussing me with friends and relatives as the "difficult one" in the family. Rarely, it seemed, did these people stop to wonder whether I was being mistreated. But then, why should they? To the outsider, my parents were such lovely people.

Father was not interested in pursuing a line of enquiry which could have exonerated me. Instead, he rang Mrs. Lamont.

"It's as I expected!" he snapped, slamming down the phone. "She said you were disrespectful."

In a fury he then applied the cane. I was in my usual position, bent over his bed.

"I'll belt the devil out of you yet," he said. I detested Mrs.

Lamont at that moment with a ferocity that I usually reserved for Father.

With the memory of the pain inflicted on my body, I peered along the street, but could not see any sign of my enemy in the garden. As we passed the house, I was too afraid to look up at the windows in case I saw that treacherous face again. I took a deep breath, and we walked the rest of the mile in silence.

Entering the school gate, he grabbed me again.

"We'll stay here all day if necessary," he threatened. "You're going to find that cardigan, if that's the last thing you ever do."

I looked at the empty school ground, and my heart sank. What if someone had stolen the cardigan? Would Father leave me there all night?

We walked up the steps and along the corridor. It seemed so bare without school bags and caps hanging on the rows of hooks, and in the stillness our footsteps echoed. I went into my classroom, with Father waiting at the door, like a lion at the mouth of a cage. The cardigan was not on the shelf under my desk. I checked all the other desks and the teacher's drawer and cupboard, but there was no sign of it.

We went underneath the school. It was dark in places, and I felt along the bench seats. My hand touched a woolly object. Excitedly I ran out into the daylight, only to discover that it was a boy's grey pullover. I was close to tears.

"You'd better find it," said Father, "or you'll be sorry."

Sorry? I thought. *My whole life is spent being sorry. Perhaps I should just apologize for existing.*

The next stop was the girls' toilets. Again, Father waited outside. Each time I emerged empty-handed, his face grew fiercer. I then thought of the playground. Most of it was open space, but there was long grass near the fence. I walked through it, bending down and parting it with my hands. Nettles stung my skin and I bumped into a tree. As I straightened to rub my head, I noticed a small patch of red between the tree trunk and the fence. Quickly I pulled at it, and out came my cardigan, covered with leaves and dirt. I pressed it tightly to my chest as though greeting a lost friend. I looked into Father's face as I showed him the cardigan, hoping to see just the slightest change of expression. There was none.

"This is not the end of it," he said. "I'm going to give you a father of a thrashing when we get home."

On the way back, I thought only of the punishment that awaited me until we approached Mrs. Lamont's house. There she was, leaning on the front fence, a horrible grin on her face. She had obviously assessed the situation well.

"Looks like you've got a little matter to attend to," she said with heavy sarcasm. Father gave a hollow laugh.

"You bet I have," he said, almost with glee.

At that moment, something deep within me changed. Until then, I had believed Father had at least enough respect for me to confine his punishments to the home. But to humiliate me publicly, in front of this dreadful woman, was an affront I would never forget. I was quiet. I was still. I just took the beating, but a part of me was not there. Father had broken my trust in the cruelest way of all.

From that moment, and for the rest of my life, I would fulfill my outward obligations as a member of the family, but never again would I allow my father to have access to my soul.

CHAPTER 6

Trying to Please God

During the next few years, Mother gave birth to two lovely daughters, Ruth and Jennifer. Each time she was pregnant, our parents prayed the baby would be a boy, but by the time Jennifer arrived, Father seemed to have accepted his fate. "All we can ever produce in this family is girls," he would say. He either did not know, or could not face the fact that he was biologically responsible for the gender of his children. Everything that went wrong was always someone else's fault, but this time he couldn't find anyone to blame—except God of course. Perhaps the Almighty was teaching him a lesson through this painful deprivation.

In my parents' eyes, I exhibited characteristics that were never seen in my sisters. Although they did not escape physical punishments entirely, the episodes of my father's cruelty in their lives were comparatively rare. Because they could see what was happening to me they seemed to develop a capacity to monitor their behavior.

"What does Father do when he goes to work?" I asked Mother one morning.

"He organizes meetings during the week," she said. "Then on some Sundays he conducts evangelistic services."

"What are they?"

"Well, you know that Jesus died on the cross so we could be forgiven. A lot of people don't know that—or they don't know that they have to accept him into their hearts."

"But don't ordinary ministers tell people that?"

"They do, but they don't go far enough. They should invite people to do something publicly, such as walking to the front of the church in a service, so everyone will know their decision. That's what God expects."

"But supposing people ask Jesus into their heart and don't do anything else. Are they forgiven?"

"I don't think they are," said Mother.

I wanted to be forgiven. I was so bad, according to Father, I needed to be. Yet every night when Mother prayed with us, and we asked God to forgive us, she never suggested that God did not hear our prayer. So were we just practicing for the day when we could be in a service and do something for other people to see?

That afternoon Mother pulled out her starched linen table cloth from the sideboard. She rolled up the matching serviettes and placed them in broad silver rings engraved with the initials of her father's family. She had spent an hour polishing her best cutlery, which she removed from felt-layered segments in a dark-green box.

"Who are the posh visitors we're having?"

"Mr. and Mrs. Benson."

I might have guessed. The Bensons were "very comfortable," Mother had said, and she liked to keep her best ware for special occasions. The couple knew Mother from her single days at the Gospel Hall, where Mr. Benson was the senior elder.

The Mercedes Benz glided on to the footpath, looking out of place in the humble surroundings. Our front door was open, and we could smell Mrs. Benson's perfume as she walked down the path. Deborah and I peered through the blinds in our bedroom to see all the sparkling jewelry she was wearing. Mother and Father went to the door to greet them.

"May the blessing of God rest upon this home," said Mr. Benson, sounding like the Archbishop of Canterbury.

"We're so delighted to have you," said Mother in her charming manner.

"God has honored us with your presence," Father added. Deborah and I looked at each other and started to giggle. We waited for a few minutes, and when we thought it was safe to do so, we emerged, trying to look as solemn as the occasion required.

"Would you be good enough to ask the Lord's blessing on our gathering?" said Father when we had taken our places at the table. Father had been known to offer up an extended grace before a meal, but he was no match for Mr. Benson, who interspersed his lengthy prayer with various biblical quotations and exhortations. I pressed my hand hard over my mouth, trying to stifle my laughter. I sneaked a look at Deborah, but she seemed to be concentrating on the flow of words from the great man.

Father always dominated conversations at meal times, but he was silent in Mr. Benson's presence, just uttering the occasional "Amen to that." We adjourned to the lounge, and Mr. Benson opened the large Bible he had brought with him. He read from the book of Proverbs, "My son, hear the instruction of thy father, and forsake not the law of thy mother." There was not much chance of avoiding either of those admonitions in our home. Mr. Benson then told the gathering about the wisdom God had given him.

"Do you hear the goodly words that proceed from my lips?" he asked.

"Indeed we do," said Father. "We are so blessed."

Jennifer was lying in her bassinet near Mother. Mr. Benson stood up and extended both arms out in front of him.

"Hand me your infant," he said to Mother. "I want to present her to God." Mother complied, but I could tell by the look on her face she thought Mr. Benson was taking things a bit far.

After another long prayer, in which he could have been a Hebrew patriarch pronouncing the blessing on his eldest son, he handed Jennifer to Father, who decided to add his own blessing on our baby sister. Jennifer had been baptized the previous Sunday, and it seemed to me she was the most prayed-for child in Australia!

We were all still standing for the impromptu ceremony, and I thought we were about to sit when Mr. Benson looked into my eyes for several seconds. He then placed his right hand on top of my head.

"I feel the Spirit in your eldest daughter," he said.

Mother and Father looked at each other in dismay. Surely the godly man could not have made such a terrible mistake.

"That is so gracious of you," said Father. "I'm sure Lynne will remember this moment for the rest of her life."

"Yes, I will, Mr. Benson." I tried my hardest to sound over-whelmed.

"I've got the Spirit!" I said to Deborah later that night after the Bensons had gone. "You'll have to treat me with respect." We both rolled on our beds with laughter.

The following week in place of Sunday School, we had a visit from a children's speaker. It was the first time I had ever been into the church building. It was so much bigger than the Sunday School hall, with beautiful stained-glass windows and a huge platform stretched across the front of the building. A window in the center of the back wall allowed a stream of light to flood the area behind the pulpit. This stood so high that I thought people would get stiff necks looking up at the preacher.

Mr. McIntyre, the visiting speaker, did not go up to the pulpit. He had erected a little stage between the front pews and the platform surrounded by curtains along the top and sides. A few assistants stood behind the stage. When we were all seated, he gave us a big smile.

"It's so good to see all your happy faces," he said. I didn't think my face looked particularly happy, but I tried to smile to make him feel good. He moved closer to his little stage.

"Once upon a time," he began, "a man had two sons whom he loved very much." The assistants put their hands behind the curtains, and three figures on the end of strings walked jerkily out. The oldest one stuck out two bony arms to put them around the two younger ones. I tried to imagine Father doing that to us!

"One day, the younger son said to his father, 'Give me my share of the property.' The father did so, and soon afterward, the son went into a distant country and spent all his money doing wild things." There were figures at a party on the stage, lying all over each other. I think they were supposed to be drunk. In our church, nobody ever touched alcohol.

"When all his money had gone, there was a famine, and the son took a job feeding pigs." Little round pink things scuffled onto the stage, and the figure on the strings waved his arm towards them in a throwing action.

"The son was very hungry and wanted to eat the pigs' food, but he was not allowed to." The figure lay down, putting his hand on his stomach.

"'I must be mad', he said to himself. 'At home, the servants have plenty of food. I will go home and tell Father that I have sinned and don't deserve to be his son but I would like him to employ me as a servant.'" The figure got up and hobbled out behind the left curtain.

"The son arrived home and spoke to his father as he had planned, but the father said to his servants, 'Bring the best robe and put it on my son. Put a ring on his finger, and sandals on his feet. Let's kill our best calf and have a feast. My son was lost, but he is found.'" There was another party scene, but all the figures were sitting or standing upright this time.

"The older brother was angry. 'You have never given me a feast' he said, 'and I've served you faithfully all these years.' But the father said, 'Everything I own is now yours. We thought your brother was dead, but he is alive again. We're celebrating his return.'" The older son bounced off the stage while the party continued.

"Each one of us is like that younger son," said Mr. McIntyre. "We have all gone away from our heavenly Father. We have all sinned."

Oh no! I thought. *He's not going to talk about sin. It's all I ever seem to hear.* Then he told us about Jesus and how we must invite him into our hearts. I had lost count of the number of times I had done that, lying in my bed at night.

"I'm going to ask you to pray a prayer with me," continued Mr. McIntyre, "and if you really mean the words, I want you to come down the front here, and I will talk to you and give you a little book." We all prayed the prayer.

"Come forward now," he said, "while our eyes are still closed."

Several children in my pew got straight up and walked towards him. Would I join them? I didn't know what to do. I stood up, then sat down again. I thought of the conversation I'd had with Mother about the need to do something publicly at a service. Of course! This was my opportunity. Some older children from the back also came down the aisles, and before long it seemed that every child in the building was at the front, all squashed together. I stood up again and walked out to join them. I had done it! I was now accepted by God. I was his child.

As soon as the meeting was over, I raced home. "You know what you said about doing something at a service to show people you've accepted Jesus?"

"Yes," said Mother, uncertainly.

"Well, I did it this morning—at the children's service."

"Oh," she said, her voice dropping.

"Aren't you pleased?" I looked at her in despair.

"Yes, of course I am. But you're a bit young for that. One day when you're older, you'll have another opportunity and it will mean more to you then."

I could not win. Everything I did was wrong—even responding to an invitation in church. Was I so bad that even my good actions were unacceptable? How many more years would I have to wait before I was regarded as a child of God—both by my parents and the Church?

Of course, I should have thought of it—the church!

"Mother, you told me that when a baby is baptized, she becomes a member of God's family. That must mean I have been accepted by God."

"Most people believe that," said Mother. "But your father and I think it just means you belong to the family of the church. It does not affect your situation with God."

In bed that night I said to God, "I'm tired of asking to be your child. I've done everything I possibly can to get it right. If there's anything more I have to do, you'll have to show me." I fell asleep in a state of anger towards God and all his human representatives.

CHAPTER 7

A Family Holiday

The August school holidays were approaching. We had always spent them at Mooloolaba, where the rental was cheap and the fishing was good. But this year we were going to try Caloundra.

"Perhaps we could invite my mother to come with us," said Father. "She gets on well with the whole family."

"Yes... she does," said Mother. "But we could hardly invite her without inviting Mum. I'd never hear the end of it."

"Your mum sets people against each other. She causes trouble wherever she goes." Father was right; Grandma Denham had a very nasty streak that had often reduced her daughter to tears. Still, I felt Father was not in a position to sit in judgment on anyone else.

"So it's either both of them or none," Mother added. "I don't think having both of them would work, but of course, it's up to you."

"Let's take both. Perhaps I can mediate between them."

I smiled to myself. *Father—a mediator?*

We could not all fit in the car, so Father took the Grandmas and the younger ones. The rest of us caught the train to Landsborough, where he picked us up later.

"I can always smooth things over in the office," he said, "but those two!" Mother refrained from comment, but her look of resignation filled me with anger. Once more, her wisdom had been ignored.

At the house, Grandma Denham had made the adults cups of tea. "This one's for you," she said to Mother, placing a cup and saucer at the end of the table.

"That's Peter's position, Mrs. Denham," said Grandma Lewis. "*He's* the head of the family."

"Mrs. Lewis!" snapped Grandma Denham. "*I* made the tea. *I* will decide where everyone sits."

Mother sat at the end of the table as Father walked in.

"Would you mind sitting at the side, just for now?" whispered Mother. Father did not seem inclined to make an issue of it. He had obviously bitten off more than he could chew. It was one thing to have a family of five females whom he controlled completely, but quite another to have two strong-willed women who were well able to dominate him.

Grandma Denham and Mother prepared the evening meal, while Grandma Lewis went to her room, where Deborah and I were playing a game on the floor.

"Do you want us to leave?" I asked.

"No, I'm just going to rest. I'm rather tired. I had a bad night." Deborah and I looked at each other, trying to keep a straight face. Grandma was always having bad nights. "I didn't sleep a wink" she would say. A few months earlier we had asked her, "What keeps you awake?"

"It's your Uncle Angus. He gives me the knocks."

"Does he knock on the wall?" I was picturing our emotionally retarded uncle banging his fists in despair. He detested his mother-in-law, but he and my aunt and their children were forced to stay with Grandma Lewis for financial reasons.

"No. But he's such an evil person, his spirit makes the whole house shake."

"Oh, Gran!" I said, unable to restrain my laughter. One thing about Grandma Lewis, she never took offence.

"I've been reading about him in the Psalms." She reached under her pillow and pulled out a well-worn Bible. "Here it is. David is talking about the enemies of God. 'Let them be confounded and troubled for ever. Let them be put to shame and perish.' That's what'll happen to your uncle if he doesn't mend his ways."

"Mrs. Lewis, would it be *too* much trouble for you to set the table?" Grandma Denham stuck her head around the bedroom door.

"Mum's feeling tired," said Father, overhearing the conversation. "She'll probably help you later."

Grandma Denham swung around. "And who made *you* an authority on the matter? Your mother is just reading the Bible. There's nothing wrong with her."

"You're just like Martha in the scriptures," Father sighed, "rushing around, doing all these secondary things. But remember, Jesus commended Mary. She just wanted to sit at his feet and listen." Grandma glared at Father and strode back into the kitchen.

Father never spoke about his childhood, but we picked up bits of information from Mother. Our grandfather, whom we never knew, was raised in a violent family and believed he had to whip his son into shape. The fierce conflicts that arose due to my grandfather's attitude were made even worse by my father's relationship with his mother. She completely dominated both her children as well as her husband. My father was also made painfully aware that his parents favored his sister. Apart from his fundamental hostility to females, I came to believe my father's rejection of me was based on an underlying fear that even as a child I could somehow control him the way his mother had done. Fortunately for my sisters, my father saw no evidence in them of any desire to dominate him.

It was not only Grandma's personality that could be terrifying, but her physical presence. She was tall and straight and weighed 240 pounds. Folds of surplus flesh hung down from her jawline, touching the rolls in her sagging neck. Her body was shaped like a barrel, with mountainous breasts supported by a circular stomach. We had visited her recently.

"Well, how's my boy?" she had greeted Father at the top of her creaky stairs.

"How many times do I have to tell you? I'm not your 'boy.' I'm your son."

"You've lost weight," she said.

"I'm the same weight I've been for the past twenty years," Father snapped.

"You need something to eat." Grandma seemed to believe that a statement from anyone other than herself was not part of reality.

"We've just had a hot dinner!" said Mother, who usually avoided visiting her mother-in-law. It wasn't that Grandma was unkind to her, but Mother said she had never felt accepted by Father's parents. Grandfather had even refused her permission to teach at Sunday School because she attended dances at the YWCA.

"You can all come into the kitchen," said Grandma, putting her arms around us and pushing us through the door. "You sit there, and you sit there." Father obeyed. Mother eventually sat down, probably afraid of his reaction if she refused.

"I've just made some fairy cakes," said Grandma, bringing out a huge tin from the cupboard.

She was to live to eighty-four, defying medical wisdom in having spent most of her waking hours with cakes and biscuits. She piled several of the former onto each of our plates. Mother's arm did not move. Father picked one up, took a small bite, and

54

then replaced it. Deborah ate all hers, but I followed Mother's lead.

"Come on, Lynne," said Grandma, munching her fourth cake. "Eat up. You look so thin."

"I'm terribly sorry, Gran," I said, "but I've just had a huge meal. You know what a wonderful cook Mother is," I added, looking across at the pecked-at cake on Father's plate.

"How are things at the church, Mum?" he asked.

"A neighbor is minding the little ones," Mother interrupted. "We should be going home."

As I thought back on that meaningless encounter, I felt I understood Father a little better. But then I wondered why he would engage in the sort of behavior he could not tolerate in his own mother.

The following morning we attended the local church. At the entrance door, a man with his head held high and shoulders back smiled at us through a closely-clipped, orange-brown mustache. The bar of ribbons he wore suggested he was a retired Army man. "Welcome to Caloundra," he said briskly, presenting us each with a hymn book.

A few elderly ladies were seated toward the back, one of them with her feet resting on a large cushion on the floor. The eight of us just fitted into one pew, a short distance in front of them. The only other person in the building was the organist, who seemed about the same age as the ladies behind us. Her back was to the congregation, her pelvis occupying most of the organ stool. She wobbled from side to side as she alternately pressed two rectangular pedals at the base of the organ, which pumped air to create the sound. To my ears, it was an awful, scratchy noise—like a piano accordion.

The minister entered through a door in the back wall and walked quietly up the steps into the pulpit. When he looked down at the congregation, the upper edges of his rimless, half-moon glasses seemed to cut his eyes in two. A clerical collar was wrapped around his plump, short neck, rubbing against his chin.

"It's lovely to see you all here," he said, "particularly our visitors." Since we made up more than half the congregation, I felt the welcome was sincere.

"Some of the Lord's people are on holidays," he continued, "but I know they are with us in spirit."

Hearing that phrase reminded me of a comment by our minister at Walka: "I prefer spooks with boots and socks on."

"It's difficult to preach to a timber yard," the minister continued. "Do you think you could all come forward and fill up the gaps." I couldn't work out how two rows of bodies could fill any gap, but we did as he asked. The Army man came in from the porch and sat at the back.

After a short prayer, the minister announced the first hymn, "Now thank we all our God." The organist struggled through the introduction at a slow pace, but since it was a stately tune, the speed seemed appropriate. We began to sing, but something was wrong. By the time we reached the end of the first line, the booming voice of the Army man was halfway through the second line. He was singing it in march tempo! Grandma Lewis had an enormous voice and managed to keep the rest of us in time with the organist, but the Army man went on regardless. At the end of the verse, the minister stopped us.

"Perhaps, Miss Murgatroyd, you could play the hymn just a shade faster, and we'll all try to keep up with you," he added, looking straight at the lone figure in the back seat. I wondered whether the Army man might be deaf, but then I thought he was probably like Father—always needing to be in charge.

At the beginning of the sermon, the organist moved away from the organ and sat in the front pew. The minister had a sing-song voice and before long I noticed the organist's head starting to nod. She jerked it back up a few times, but then it stayed down. After twenty minutes of nothing in particular, the minister announced the final hymn. But the organist did not move. He repeated the announcement in a slightly louder voice. Still there was no response.

"Miss Murgatroyd!" The unfortunate woman let out a cry and shook her head violently.

"Oh!" she said, looking up into the pulpit, "I'm so sorry." As she rushed across to the organ, I wondered whether this might be a regular occurrence with a person of that age. It was sad to see a church in decline. I assumed most of the absent members were of similar vintage. Occasionally, I would hear of churches that had to close. Father always fought to keep them open, saying there would always be growth if ministers preached the gospel faithfully. He refused to accept that some were simply not talented as public speakers. Father had a habit of expecting the impossible.

As I was shaking the minister's hand after the service, I asked him if there was a piano where I could practice. The previous year Father had bought a second-hand piano, and I was making reasonable progress as a student.

"There's one in the hall," he said, pointing to a weatherboard building with the paintwork flaking. "It's not exactly a Steinway, but you're welcome to use it at any time. The door is left open."

"Can I try it now?" I asked Mother.

"I want to go straight home," said Grandma Lewis, in a tone of voice that was not to be challenged.

"She's had another bad night!" Deborah whispered.

I walked back to the church early the next morning, carrying my music case. The open hall door did not even have a lock. At the far end of the hall was a stage, where, in the distant past, some aspiring young actor might have made a first trembling entrance. All that remained were two faded green curtains, half falling from the overhead rods. Holes and rips made a mockery of their once proud role in stimulating the audience's imagination.

The piano sat at the foot of the stage. The lid was resting sideways on top of it, like a piece of dumped baggage. I tried to put it back in its correct position, but parts of the hinges were twisted, and it would not fit. Rather than risk the thing falling on top of me, I leaned it against a wall. The light bulb above the piano had been smashed, but there was almost enough light from a nearby window. It was covered in dirt and cobwebs, and the lower pane had jammed shut. Before cleaning the window in the hope of getting a bit more light, I checked to see if there were any spiders. The webs, however, seemed to be as old as the hall, the creator spider probably living only in the spirit of its descendants.

The piano keys were a dull yellow, with dark streaks running parallel to the edges. Some of the keys had lost their veneers, leaving a surface rough to the touch. I played some scales, but a few of the notes did not sound. A passer-by might have thought I was missing one or two of my fingers. The squeak of the sustaining pedal was so loud and the action so stiff I decided not to use it. Was it really worthwhile continuing?

Had I been a normal child, I probably would have given up at that point. Then again, I would almost certainly have given the whole thing a miss during the holidays. Father had not made any ruling on it. But something deep inside me would not let me rest. I had to strive and strive—to become better and better. *Was I aiming for an impossible standard I had set myself, or was I trying to please Father, against all my instincts?* I did not know. I just had to keep going.

In the middle of a piece I heard the sound of a bouncing ball. A few boys in swimsuits, covered in sand, had come into the hall. They threw the ball in all directions, and it bounced off the walls like a slow squash ball. It was a wonder there were any windows left. I felt like asking them to leave, but it was always important for me not to spoil the church's image. Then the ball landed on the piano where the lid should have been and bounced down onto the keys.

"We're terribly sorry," said one of the boys.

"That's all right," I said cheerily. "Would you like to have a play?"

"Yeah, let's!"

They banged their way from the top to the bottom, then ran outside for a new adventure. They were so carefree. Part of me wanted to be like that, but I knew I was different.

The house we were renting was at Bulcock Beach, and after breakfast, Deborah, Ruth and I went out with Father and reached the sandbanks.

"Form a semi-circle around here," he said. "You have to be quick." He plunged a large metal pump deep into the sand, pulled it up, and spread its contents near our feet. We bent down and dug our hands into the yellow and grey sand.

"Ouch!" said Ruth, as the claw of a yabby nipped her finger.

"Quick, grab it!" The small crayfish dug its way back into the sand, but it could not escape Father's groping hand as he held it by its claw and dropped it, helpless, into a bucket of water. I felt for that yabby as it struggled to crawl up the side of the bucket. It was just as much Father's prisoner as I was. All our struggling achieved nothing.

Later that day, with a large supply of yabbies and some prawns, the four of us pushed off in a rowing boat. We anchored some distance out into the channel that ran between the coast and the northern end of Bribie Island. Far out in the open sea, two bronze-colored oil tankers broke the straight line of the horizon. A strong breeze coming in from the ocean was chopping the calmer waters of the channel, making it seem like a continuation of the great deep rather than a quiet place for family recreation.

Each of us had a fishing line wrapped around the thick end of a narrow-necked bottle. Father threaded the bait on and threw our lines out.

"Whatever you do, don't pull the line when you feel a bite. You don't want to frighten the fish. They have to believe the bait is harmless." He then used a rod to cast his own line out a long way further than our little ones could reach.

"I've got a bite," said Ruth, dropping her bottle in excitement.

"Here, I'll take it." Father took the bottle and handed me his rod. I felt honored to be holding such a prized possession. After several minutes, he pulled the line towards him in a sharp movement and began to wind it around the bottle.

"I've got him," said Father, standing up. We looked out beyond the end of the line and a wriggling white shape was creating a different kind of disturbance on the channel's surface from that produced by the wind. The fish fought with all its might as it was pulled closer and closer to the edge of the boat. But it might as well have given up then. Father would not be denied. He placed the bottle on the floor of the boat so he could use both hands to regulate the pull of the line. A medium-sized bream was raised in triumph over the edge of the boat, its scales glistening in the afternoon sun. Then it fell with a thud into the center of the boat, where it thrashed around in a small pool of water. Father removed the hook from its mouth and placed it in a hessian bag.

In the meantime, I was feeling a bite on Father's line, and before long he began reeling it in. Whenever we went fishing, Father always seemed to catch more than anyone else in the area, though on that afternoon we were the only people with lines. All we saw were a few outboard motors doing the length of the channel.

"This is strange," said Father. "With the fish biting, you'd think everyone would be out." He leant over the edge of the boat and put his hand in the water.

"I don't like the feel of this. The current wasn't nearly this strong a short time ago. I'm going to pull up the anchor. Sit in the middle of the boat."

He moved forward to where the anchor chain was attached. With the strong current, the boat was pulling away from the point where the chain disappeared below the water. He pulled at the chain and the boat moved till it seemed to be directly above the anchor. Again he pulled, but the anchor was stuck. Standing up, he made one final attempt. The boat tilted forward.

"We're in trouble," he said. "It won't move. I'm going to pray." He bowed his head for a few moments while we held on to each other.

"I'm going to try to row to the side of it," he said.

He and I swapped places and he grabbed the oars, pulling hard on one side. For a while we didn't seem to be moving, but with perspiration dripping from his forehead, he made an almighty effort and the position of the boat changed slightly.

"Hold this oar down in the water," he said to me. "You'll need both hands."

"Deborah can help me," I said, knowing how much stronger her hands were than mine. We both held on with all our might. Father made several pulls at the anchor. Then it suddenly released, throwing him backwards. The boat lurched dangerously to one side. We grabbed each other in fear. Father's head caught the edge of a tin we used for bailing out, and his forehead began to bleed. Staggering to an upright position he motioned to us to return to our seats as he took both oars.

Although we were not a huge distance from the shore, we were making no progress against the current. A few days earlier I saw a large sign that read, "You who go out in boats, keep well away from the bar." I had asked Mother, "Do fishermen and sailors often get drunk?" Mother was a member of the Queensland Temperance League, and I knew she was an authority on the subject of drinking.

"No," she said with a smile. "That sign's about the sand bar between the tip of Bribie Island and the mainland. It's dangerous for small boats."

As I thought about that conversation and how small our boat was, I became very frightened that we could be swept out to the bar. What would Father do then? Could his prayers rescue us? I didn't say anything, but I looked at the position of our boat in relation to a point on the shore. Although we were making no headway, the current was actually taking us away from the bar. I almost cried with relief. I was terrified of the water. Several people had tried to teach me to swim, but I could never trust my body or the water. I would just freeze.

Father stopped rowing. He was exhausted. Blood was streaming from his forehead. We drifted … and drifted … I looked anxiously at where we were heading. A rocky edge formed the shoreline further along. Although we would probably just miss that, we would almost certainly collide with rocks under the surface if we drifted any further in.

Across on land, people were lying in the sun or strolling along the Esplanade, unaware that there was no one in control of our boat. Father showed no interest in calling out for help. Perhaps he did not have the strength.

"Do you want us to yell out?" I asked him. He shook his head weakly. Then in a superhuman effort, he gripped the oars with all his strength and drove them down into the swirl, defying the might of the raging waters. After each stroke, he let out a gasp. Just when I felt he would have to give up the struggle, we stopped suddenly. The nose of the boat had stuck in some sand. Deborah and I quickly jumped over the side, Father lifted Ruth up, and we waded to the shore.

That night I thought about the strength and courage Father had shown. I also had to admire the strength of his convictions, even though most of them seemed to be so wrong. If only that strength could be used to uplift and inspire us, his children. If only he could believe in us, could accept that we, too, were made in the image of God, that even daughters could enrich his life beyond measure. In closing himself off to those possibilities, he was depriving himself of the real joy of fatherhood.

CHAPTER 8

Father Always Wins

"They're having a session on softball after school today," I said to Mother. "I think I'll have a go at it." This was a new challenge. I had never played sport before, but already I could picture myself hitting the ball really hard—perhaps finishing up as captain of the team. I packed my sandshoes and waved her a cheery goodbye.

By some miracle I managed to behave well in class that day. I was not going to risk being kept in and miss my opportunity. At three o'clock, all the girls ran down the steps, changed their shoes, and met Miss Ralph, the slim, quietly-spoken sports mistress. We pushed each other to try to get close to her.

She led us across to the playing area and explained the field positions. "Who'd like to go on a base?" There were no volunteers.

"Everyone to my right will field." Miss Ralph extended her arm and brought it down between the shoulders of two girls wedged close together. "Those to my left can line up to bat."

We took our positions, and the first girl in the line-up strode out. She grabbed the bat and flung it across her shoulder. Her solid arms delivered a deadly blow to the ball, which beat the field and came to rest in the grass near the fence. It looked so easy. I would hit the ball right over the fence. Miss Ralph pitched and I took a wild swing. The ball passed me by, disdainful of my presence.

"Don't worry. We'll try again." The sports mistress pitched as gently as she could, again and again, but I could not connect with a single ball.

"It will be easier next time," said Miss Ralph, giving me a reassuring smile.

Next time! How could I ever face it again? Already I knew the other girls had written me off as stupid. Watching everyone carefully, I crept backward. The fielders couldn't see me, nor could Miss Ralph, as I sneaked away and hid underneath the school. "I will never play sport again," I said, flinging my sandshoes in my bag.

"You're home early." Mother was bringing in some clothes from the line.

"Well, I didn't like it much." I strode to the piano. "Anyway, I can beat them all at this," I whispered so Mother couldn't hear. Gritting my teeth, I raced up and down the scales.

My failure on the sporting field did not diminish my enthusiasm as a follower of cricket. Father had introduced me to radio broadcasts at a young age. Perhaps he was trying to alleviate the pain of not having a son with whom to share his passion. When the Australian team was batting, I used the counter at the end of my knitting needle—not to count the number of rows I had completed, but to register my team's score.

I drew an oval on a sheet of paper and a rectangle in the middle for the pitch. "Could you put a dot to show me where 'fine leg' is?" Father did so, and explained all the positions on the field, together with their subtle variations.

Australia was playing a test match at the Adelaide Oval in a series against England. Arthur Morris, our great opening batsman, had been having problems with the bowling of England's Alec Bedser. I sat on a chair in the lounge opposite the radio. Father switched it on for the pre-match commentary.

"*Morris doesn't seem to be able to read Bedser,*" said the commentator in an anxious voice.

"*Yes. It's almost as though the medium-pacer has a hoodoo on the opener.*"

I did not like the sound of this. "Do you think Morris will get through the opening session?"

"It's an easy-paced pitch," said Father. "He should be OK."

"*They're setting an attacking field.*" The commentator's tone added to the tension. I curled up on the chair. My heart was thumping. "*In comes Bedser bowling to Morris.*" I leaped up from the chair and ran out of the room.

"What's wrong with you?" Father shouted.

"I can't stand it. He might get out."

"You're a bad sport. You have to win all the time, don't you?"

I did not reply. For the only time I could ever remember, Father was right. I hated being the way I was, but the fear that one of my players could fail was too much. I ran to the bedroom and put on some shoes.

"I'll be back later," I called out.

Walking quickly down the middle of the street, I tried to avoid the sound of radios. At the bottom of the hill, there was bushland. My pace slowed as I walked along the winding dirt track. Lorikeet and currawong birds were forming a chorus with the cicadas. I stopped to listen and to take in the stillness. My pulse rate, which had soared at the thought of an Australian batsman losing his wicket, was gradually lowered with the soothing bush sounds. The thick foliage of the tall trees created a blanket against the sun, and the track in places was an obstacle course of puddles. I tried to leap across the biggest one, falling short by only a few inches and splashing my leg with mud. I plucked off a flower and smelt its fragrance, then ran my fingers along a mossy ridge and wiped the moisture over my face.

Beyond the trees was a creek surrounded by sand hills. It was a beautiful secluded place, except for a food processing plant on the far side. During operational hours the smells belied the rustic aura of the setting. The area was usually deserted, and I was grateful for the solitude.

After taking my shoes off, I lay down on the grass and looked up at the faint streaks of white cloud across the pale sky. A soft breeze fanned my face and a small bird settled nearby. I could faintly hear the sounds of the creek falling over the rocks, and in my dreamlike state I almost forgot about the cricket.

The stillness and the view of the heavens were eventually interrupted by a plane on its way to the Eagle Farm Aerodrome, jolting me back into the world of action. *I wonder what the score is. I must get back home and find out.* I ran back along the track and up the hill.

Arthur Morris was on his way to a double century. I was ecstatic. But if only I'd stayed home, I could have heard the descriptions and listened to Johnny Moyes, the specialist commentator, analyzing the skills of our batsmen.

A few weeks earlier, I had gone outside to collect 'The Courier Mail.' Quickly I opened the sports section to read about my heroes. "What's this special supplement?" I called out to anyone who could hear me. "Look at this! Big photos of all our team!" I rushed into the kitchen to show Mother. Although she was not interested in cricket, I always wanted to share my joys with her.

"Can I cut them out?"

"You'll have to ask your father."

"Only after I've read both sides." He proceeded to read every word, while I jumped up and down beside his chair.

He finished at last. I borrowed Mother's dressmaking scissors and carefully cut around each picture and the summary of the player's history below. Then I taped the pictures around my bedroom wall, placing them in batting order. Lindsay Hassett, the captain, was No. 4, and I put him in a slightly elevated position, giving him the recognition I felt he deserved. I thought Neil Harvey was a magnificent batsman, and that Ray Lindwall was the greatest bowler in the world, but my favorite player was Keith Miller, the brilliant allrounder. There was an exuberance about him that I found irresistible.

"He can do everything," I said, looking admiringly at his photo. "That makes him the best."

I wondered why I was so fiercely competitive—at least when it came to supporting my team. Perhaps at some level I was competing with my father—in an impossible game where God had ensured that he would always win. Even on those rare occasions where we shared an interest, my father's comments would inevitably cause me to criticize myself, reinforcing my belief in my own unworthiness in the eyes of God.

CHAPTER 9

Showing off at School

The temperature was 98 degrees. Small groups of children straggled across the playground. The handrails were too hot to hold as we lugged our suitcases up the steps. Early morning games were forgotten as young bodies soon drifted down to the cooler concrete floor underneath the school.

At nine o'clock the gong sounded from the school veranda. Four hundred children lined up listlessly, seniors at the back, juniors at the front. We turned our heads to the left on command, where two pairs of small hands pulled on the long white rope. The kettle drums rattled, the chins in the front rows tilted upwards as the Australian flag struggled to the top of the white pole. Reluctant to show its brilliant colors, it hung like a wrung-out dishrag. The only currents of air that day were in the stratosphere.

"Salute the flag," Mr. Wilkes, the headmaster, barked from the platform at the top of the steps. Hundreds of hands touched hundreds of right eyebrows, then slapped down to their thighs. The fife and drum band lined up at right angles to the parade blew and banged its way through the National Anthem. The Lord's Prayer was recited in a monotone. The speed of the address to the Almighty seemed to increase throughout the year with each rendition.

Stillness of body was expected from each child. "That boy at the end of the fourth row." Mr. Wilkes' arm indicated the position of the offender. "You were wriggling. Come out here. And that girl in the back with the green blouse. You were talking. I could see you. Out!" Each morning a collection of wrigglers and talkers was captured in the disciplinary net, and stood facing the assembly of non-offenders.

"Stand at ease." There was not much of that under the burning sky, but stiff limbs took advantage of the respite. "Atten—shun!" The girls' shoes clicked together, the boys dragged their feet through the dirt.

"Now listen carefully." The headmaster spoke about the polio epidemic, lost property, bikes being stolen from underneath the school, and arrangements for cleaning the playground. Then he straightened his long body as if preparing to announce the end of civilization.

"Pull your shoulders back. Stand tall. Hands behind." The muscular boys stuck their chests out. The adolescent girls in the back rows looked at each other and giggled. Some complied with exaggerated effect to the command, while others ignored it. "Be proud of yourselves. Be proud of your country. We are part of the glorious British Commonwealth. We are loyal subjects of King George the Sixth." On and on he droned. The exhortations seemed interminable. Rigid, hatless bodies began to wilt, dehydrating in the relentless heat. The girl next to me fainted.

This is outrageous, I thought. *Parents should complain to the authorities.* More bodies fell as teachers rushed to give aid.

"Right turn!" shouted Mr. Wilkes at the end of his ramblings. The bodies which had remained upright marched to their classes as the band played 'Men of Harlech.'

The following day I woke to the gentle touch of Mother's hand. I sat up and drank my orange juice, dreading the thought of another hot parade. Perhaps I would be the next one to faint. Mother pulled back the mosquito net and raised the blind. Deborah had drunk her orange juice, almost without waking.

Over breakfast, we told Mother again about the parades and the awful teachers at the Walka school.

"The place gets worse every day," I said. "I think we should transfer to Edenvale. The other kids in this area go there, and they love it."

"I've been thinking about that myself for some time," she said. "I'll suggest it to your father."

"No way," the voice bellowed as he strode into the kitchen. "I went to a tough school and it didn't do me any harm. In any case, if you went to Edenvale you would be able to get the bus. I'm not going to have lazy kids around the place."

My teacher was Mr. Stewart, a short man whose broad shoulders sat untidily on top of a narrow body. His top lip did not quite cover his long front teeth, giving the impression that he was always smiling. Apart from his appearance, his personality reminded me of Father's. He never missed an opportunity to shout commands, at school, either on the playground with a megaphone, or in the classroom without one.

Seating in the class was in the order of merit, and as I was usually second, I shared a desk with Victor, the top student. As far I was concerned, he was the only interesting person in the room.

It was the Monday morning mathematics lesson. "I'll be glad when I get to high school," Victor yawned. "This stuff bores me."

"Me too," I replied.

"Come out here, you two," shouted the teacher.

I led the way. Mr. Stewart smacked me several times on the leg as hard as he could. It hurt, but I was used to far worse. At home I was punished for accidents or for speaking inappropriately. At school, I could avoid punishment if I managed to be silent for six hours.

"Now your turn," he said to Victor. Boys were always hit with a

LEAVING FAITH, FINDING MEANING

ruler, unless they were sent to the headmaster. Mr. Wilkes used a long cane, which was applied to the open hand, while our teacher used a ruler in a similar manner. I watched Victor's punishment, wondering if I were partly to blame.

"Get back to your seats." Mr. Stewart stood erect. "Maybe that will keep you quiet for a while." Following the tradition for boys in that situation, Victor walked back with a swagger and a forced smile of triumph as though he had not felt a thing.

Although I was near the top of the class at the age of twelve, I was not a particularly good student. I had no love of literature, but I remember being given a book about the Inuit in my early years. The cosy inside of the igloo and the gleaming snow outside, leading down to waters of the deepest blue had fascinated me.

The only subject that really aroused my interest was English grammar. I was intrigued by verbal nouns, nouns in apposition, dangling participle phrases, and clauses as subjects and objects. That afternoon we had a grammar lesson.

"Listen to these two sentences. 'A number of people were there. A number of people was there.' Which is correct?"

A boy sitting in front of me raised his hand. "It's 'were there.'"

"No," said Mr. Stewart. " 'Number' is singular, so the verb has to be singular." When I felt it safe to do so, I leaned forward.

"You were right," I whispered.

"I heard that," said the teacher. "Would you care to explain yourself?"

"Well, actually, Sir, you could say, 'The number of people who were there was 20,' but when you use 'number' in the sense of 'several' it has to be 'were.'"

"You think you know everything, don't you? Would you like to take the class?"

"All right," I replied. I wasn't sure if he was serious, so I remained seated.

"Well, come on then," said Mr. Stewart, moving away from his desk.

I rose from my chair and walked down the aisle. I then went to the blackboard, wiped it clean, and found a piece of chalk.

"Look at her," whispered a boy in the front row. "She's game."

On the board I wrote, 'Strolling along the track, a beautiful view appeared.' Turning around I asked "What's wrong with that sentence?"

"Please, Miss, there's nothing wrong with it," said a cheeky boy at the back.

"Oh dear," I said, pretending to frown, "I must have made a mistake. Who else thinks the sentence is correct?" A few tentative hands were raised.

"What part of speech is 'strolling'?" I asked.

"A participle."

"That's right. A participle can be part of a verb. 'He was strolling along the road.' But when it's by itself, it has to be related to a noun or pronoun. Is it related to any word in the sentence on the board?"

Victor raised his hand. "Well, it's related to 'view,' but you can't have a view that's strolling along." A few titters went around the class.

"Well done," I said, giving Victor a smile. "There are two ways to correct this sentence. Victor can give us one.'

"As we were strolling along the track, a beautiful view appeared."

"That's right. Can anyone else think of another way?" There were no takers.

Mr. Stewart then came to my rescue. "Strolling along the track, we saw a beautiful view." He then stood up and I looked anxiously towards him. Had I done something wrong—perhaps taken too much of the lesson time?

"That was very well done, Lynne," he said in a conciliatory tone. "You would make an excellent teacher—unless," he added with a wry smile, "you decide to go into politics. You could argue your way out of anything!"

I was pleased with my teaching effort but puzzled about Mr. Stewart. At times I thought he hated me the way Father did. He certainly would not tolerate his authority being questioned, but occasionally he seemed to appreciate having me in the class. Grown-ups were so unpredictable. No wonder I found it hard to trust them.

At the same time, I had the horrible thought that my parents could be right. Was there something bad within me that was crying out for punishment?

CHAPTER 10

A Queen is Crowned

"We're having a raffle to raise money for the school," Mr. Wilkes bellowed at the morning parade. "Every family is expected to sell at least one book of tickets." He paused and looked at the children in the front rows. At that moment the only sound was the screeching of birds on the telegraph wires. I envied their freedom. I was caught in a trap of restrictions and prohibitions. Other children, like the birds, seemed to soar on the breezes while I banged my head against iron bars.

The previous year the school held a fancy-dress ball. On the day of the announcement, my classmate Madeline and I walked home from school.

"I'm going to the ball as a penguin," said Madeline. "What about you?"

"Our family doesn't go to things like that," I replied. "The only time we ever go out, it's to church." Entertainment such as opera, theatre, ballet—those things were 'of the world,' Father had said, and Christians must have nothing to do with them.

"Oh that's right, I forgot. You're religious, aren't you? But my family goes to church and they don't see anything wrong with it." I had put this argument to Mother.

"We have higher standards than other people," she explained.

"But it's just dressing up," I protested. "You always let us do that."

"It's not what people wear. There'd be dancing. That can lead to sin."

"What kind of sin?" I thought of various possibilities—lying, cheating, stealing—even arguing.

"You'll understand when you're older," said Mother. Even as a thirteen-year-old, statements about my age or lack of maturity made me furious. They seemed a poor substitute for a reasoned explanation. Sinfulness and I seemed destined never to part. I was always saying something sinful, doing something sinful, or wanting to do something sinful. Could I really be more evil than everybody else?

"Quick march!" said the headmaster. We obeyed the verb in the command, but not the adverb, as we straggled to our classrooms. Throughout the morning, I wondered how the raffle tickets would be distributed—perhaps at a central point in the school. At least that way, no one would know that I hadn't taken any. Gambling was another activity on my parents' banned list.

It was almost lunchtime, and there had been no mention of the raffle. I was beginning to think I had escaped, when I noticed Mr. Stewart opening a drawer.

"Put your pens down," he said, producing a pile of the dreaded tickets. "I'm going to hand these out. There'll be a prize for the family who sells the most." He walked up and down the aisles. Some children took two or three books. His black squeaky boots came towards my desk. I looked down, sensing that everyone was staring at me.

"How many books would you like?" he asked in a loud voice.

"I ... I don't think my parents will allow me to take them," I replied in a whisper.

"What!" he said. "Not even to help the school?"

I felt myself blushing, wishing I could slide under the desk and disappear.

"It's just ... that ... they don't believe in that sort of thing." I saw the peculiar looks of my classmates. A few sniggered. Why was I made to feel such a misfit? The teacher shook his head and walked away. How dare he blame me for having strange parents!

"Mr. Stewart wanted me to bring home some raffle tickets, but I didn't," I told Mother that afternoon.

"Good girl," she replied. "Those things are evil." I wanted to ask why, but having received rare approval, I would not risk losing it.

That evening I was doing my homework at the dining room table. The smell of overcooked steak hung in the hot, still air, the aromas unable to float out into the night through the small kitchen windows. The family radio, encased in a polished wooden box with fretted panels covering the speaker, stood in a corner near the doorway to the lounge. Sprawled out on the floor in front of the wireless, Deborah was teaching Jennifer how to play Monopoly. Ruth was having a bath.

The time signal for eight o'clock, an announcement of a broadcast from the City Hall, and the strains of 'God save the King' filled the room. I walked quickly across to the bathroom door, which always jammed a few inches from closure.

"That's the National Anthem," I yelled through the gap. "Are you standing up?"

"I am now," said Ruth, to the sound of a swish of bathwater.

Hearing the music, Deborah and Jennifer rose abruptly from the floor, their card game unable to compete with devotion to the House of Windsor. The four of us stood motionless until the final note. Only illness was accepted as a valid reason for non-compliance with our self-imposed ritual. Our parents did not object to our loyalty to the throne, but they considered it trivial compared to our loyalty to God and the scriptures.

With the passing of King George VI and the crowning of Princess Elizabeth as Queen, I felt part of a fairy tale history. How I would love to have been at Westminster Abbey and seen the Queen in all her coronation splendor.

"The school has made a block booking at the Walka Cinema for the film, 'A Queen is Crowned,'" Mr. Stewart announced one morning. "I expect everyone in this class to attend—even you, Lynne," he added, glaring at me. I could not bear the thought of another humiliation, but would I be allowed to go?

That afternoon I lay on my bed, thinking of a way to ask permission. *Perhaps if I promised to be good?* But that wouldn't work. I was always trying to be good. *Could I ask God to make them say 'yes'?* That was difficult because I never knew if God was on their side or mine. There had to be another way. "I've got it!" I exclaimed, leaping up. "This film is history, so it's part of my education!" I ran into the kitchen, where Mother was peeling potatoes in the stone sink.

"I know you don't allow us to go to the pictures," I said, "but supposing it was something organized by the school?" I looked anxiously into her face. There was no change of expression, so I pressed on, using all the logic at my command.

"Maybe we could make an exception in this case," was the quiet response. "After all, it was a Christian ceremony, and the royal family are God-fearing people." I jumped up and down on the linoleum, hardly able to believe that my powers of persuasion had won the day.

"Of course, we'll have to ask your father." In my excitement, I had almost forgotten that the head of the house had the power of veto. My ecstasy vanished.

"I've never been to a picture theatre in my life," he said later that evening, "and I won't have any child of mine inside one." Mother winced.

"But Peter, it's not as though there'll be anything of Hollywood shown."

"What's Hollywood?" I asked.

"The people who appear in those films lead immoral lives," Mother explained. "They're not faithful in marriage."

"The cinema is tainted by what is shown there," said Father. "We must abstain from all appearance of evil."

I was close to tears, disappointment mingling with rage. Father, it seemed, would stop at nothing in making me feel powerless. I was deprived of the right to be heard, let alone to present a reasoned argument. My only hope was Mother. Could she win against his rigid mind?

"Surely, Peter, a building full of school children to see a film of the Queen—no one could possibly see that as evil." Father was silent. He stared at the wall, his body motionless. Then he let out an angry sigh.

"Well, I'm not happy about it, but I suppose you've got a point." I flung my arms around Mother, almost knocking her over. Then I raced out of the room before Father could change his mind.

I had often ridden past the picture theatre, never imagining that I would be inside it one day. As I walked towards the building a few weeks later, I was excited, but almost frightened. What if Father was right—that there was something evil in the place?

I joined the other children at the entrance, and tried not to look like it was my first visit. The girls in my class often talked about their favorite film stars. I had no idea who they were, and was always too embarrassed to ask. We entered the foyer, and I saw pictures of scantily-clad women in advertisements for coming shows. Were these the unfaithful women Mother had told me about? The other children rushed over to the sweets stall, eager hands sliding sixpences, threepences and pennies across the counter. I stood back. I had no money, but sweets were not allowed in our family, so it didn't matter.

A few teachers tried to get the children into line, but they crowded around the entrances and, ignoring the usherettes, pushed and jostled each other down the aisles. I almost fell into a sagging canvas seat. What weird, shapeless things they were! Everyone else treated them with the familiarity of lounge chairs. Packets of assorted sweets were ripped open, some of their contents falling to the floor. A few Jaffas rolled down the slope, and children at the front bent down to collect the unexpected treasure.

I looked up in amazement at the giant screen. The only ones I had ever seen before were minute in comparison. One was at the church and was used by missionaries to show slides of their work, and the other one was at school, where they rarely got to the end of a film because the projector would break down.

As the film began, I quickly left my world of sin and punishment, swept up into a dimension of beauty and goodness. A heavenly choir, the Archbishop and other dignitaries in their magnificent robes, a congregation from all parts of the globe—countries within the British Commonwealth, republics, dictatorships. It mattered not their race or political persuasion. "God save the Queen," they shouted, and I longed to cry out with them. The richness of the pageantry, the grandeur of the Abbey, and the purity and loveliness of our sovereign filled my heart with wonder and joy.

I walked out of the building alone, oblivious to the chatter around me. The sounds of the trumpets, the choir, and the magnificent organ carried me up the long hill home. I went into my bedroom and closed the door. Unable to speak, I wanted no human contact. My Queen had been anointed by God, and in a way that I could not understand, I had been a part of it.

My devotion to Her Majesty would become for me a haven—a place free from pain and injustice. My feelings about God and my parents were confused, mixed with doubt and a sense of alienation. But my love for the Queen was of a different order. It was unconditional; it was boundless; it was eternal.

CHAPTER 11

A Local Wedding

"You can sit in the back seat of the church," said Mother, "but you must not talk."

She and Father moved towards the front, where the rows were draped at each end in white ribbons. My sisters and I sat in the seat near the door leading to the foyer. We were delighted that our parents had given us permission to see the wedding.

Arrangements of pink and white carnations in every available spot transformed the somber-looking building into a sacred garden. Two women in huge hats came and sat in front of us, blocking our view. We shifted along a bit, but then we could hardly see between the hats, which almost collided whenever their owners moved. It was not only the view that was obliterated. The delicate fragrance of the carnations was no match for the ladies' Lavender and Tweed, which stamped its pungent authority on our corner of the building.

The organist began her prelude, but the sounds of the instrument could be heard only when there was a lull in the chatter. Most of the congregation were friends of the bride, Merrilyn, whose family had been stalwarts of the church for generations. I did not know Merrilyn very well. She was one of the popular girls, whereas I was always an outsider. The bridegroom, Jo, was not interested in the Christian faith. He had attended church only once the week before the wedding. Jo had the looks of a film star and divided his time between modeling and lifesaving on the Gold

Coast. Most of the girls at the church thought he was a "catch." Mother did not agree.

"It's such a shame," she said. "Merrilyn is a lovely girl. There would have been a nice Christian young man somewhere for her."

"The parents are the problem," Father declared. "They could have stopped it."

"Merrilyn's in her twenties," said Mother. "She wouldn't need her parents' permission to get married." As a thirteen-year-old, I had not even considered that Father could one day exercise a power of veto over who I would marry.

"They should not have allowed her to go out with him." Father's statement indicated the policy he would pursue with his own daughters.

"That may have caused a rift in the family," Mother suggested. "If only she'd brought him to church, particularly when it was an evangelistic service. He might have been converted."

According to Mother and Father, the Bible said believers should only marry each other. I couldn't help thinking the whole thing was terribly harsh, particularly for girls, since there were many more of us in the church than there were potential husbands.

The minister led out the bridegroom and his attendants. Jo looked nervously around the building. Was it just wedding jitters, or did he feel uneasy, surrounded by all these religious people?

The sound of clicks and flashes of light came from the foyer. A man with his face screwed up against a black box walked backwards towards the inner door. Believing that his mind was as faithful as his camera in having mapped the layout of the place, he seemed unconcerned about the possibility of human obstruction. The clicking and flashing stopped as he moved aside to allow Merrilyn's two sisters, dressed in pink satin, to make one final check on their sister. The three girls shared a close bond. I envied Merrilyn. I was close to my sisters too, but would I ever be able to have them walking in front of me down the aisle at my own wedding?

The congregation stood for the Bridal March. Merrilyn clung to her father as though her life depended on him. He looked down at her and smiled. She looked lovingly up at him, and her whole body seemed to relax. The ceremony itself was conducted with a tasteful mix of decorum and informality, but as we walked home afterwards, all I could think about was that smile from Merrilyn's father. Approval, admiration, pride, love—it overflowed from him.

That afternoon, I lay on my bed and wondered, *did Merrilyn earn that smile because she was lucky enough to fit the model her parents wanted?* She had always won the highest praise from Mother—"What a sweet, gentle girl." But perhaps the smile came, in effect, from two hearts that accepted their child as a gift of God, regardless of the nature she had inherited. My own father believed that for a girl with my characteristics, the only hope of marriage would be with a man like him, who would "keep me under control." There was never any suggestion that such a man could love me for the person I was.

"She looks so beautiful." That's what they always said about brides. I wanted people to say that about me one day, but of course they would never say it until I was in a wedding gown. Lace over tulle— that's what I'd have. And a fluffy veil. But who would be standing near the minister, waiting for me? A man, according to the Bible, whom I would have to "honor and obey." The thought terrified me.

CHAPTER 12

Father tries to make
an Impression

"What a dreadful voice that man has!" Mother flashed her eyes towards the wireless—a look of disapproval I knew so well. She pulled out a freshly-washed dress from the laundry basket and shook an aluminum tin a few inches above the fabric. Droplets splashed through the holes in the lid. She rolled up the dress into a tight ball so the moisture could spread evenly through the garment, making it ready to iron.

"That voice," said Father, "belongs to Dr. Evatt, the Leader of the Opposition. He will be Australia's next Prime Minister." Father raised his arms behind his head and leaned back on the lounge chair. His legs were crossed, and there was a gap between his sock and the lower edge of his trousers. The skin was white, almost shiny. It looked cold. I thought of the man across the road with his olive skin. He laughed a lot, and gave his children cuddles.

But I was excited. The Labor Party might win the election! They were like me—struggling against powerful forces. Father knew all about politics. He didn't like the Prime Minister, and I didn't like him either. He had a posh voice and made fun of the Labor Party.

"Menzies represents the rich and powerful." Father's voice rose, and he paused, the way he sometimes did when preaching. "We should be on the side of the workers, the people who struggle." Mother was silent and continued her sprinkling.

It was early in May, and the Federal elections had been called for the 29th. Already we had collected several how-to-vote pamphlets from our letterbox. Mother was looking at them intently. "This man has character," she said quietly. I rushed over to see who it was, but she pulled the pamphlets away.

On Monday morning, as Deborah and I walked down the long hill to school, we saw huge posters stuck on all the telegraph posts. The first one read: VOTE O'BRIEN 1 FOR LABOR. Above the caption was the picture of a man's face. It was rough, and his nose was bent, like Mr. Russell's at church. Father said Mr. Russell used to be a boxer before he came to Christ.

The next day some of the posters had been pasted over with those of the Liberal candidate, John Henderson, a handsome man with neatly-combed glossy hair and a thin mustache. Despite his polished appearance, I convinced myself that he would have nothing else to offer.

"They've got no right to paste over the Labor man," I said to Deborah. But she was looking admiringly at Mr. Henderson.

I was still thinking about the two pictures as Mr. Stewart cleaned the board after the morning lesson. Clouds of chalk dust danced in a stream of sunlight that was deflected by his desk, lighting up the cupboard door on the wall opposite the windows. He had encouraged us to listen to parliament but had not discussed the policies of the parties.

"Although you can't vote yet," he said in a serious tone, digging his fingers into the back of his chair, "you need to know what the political parties stand for." His voice became more intense, and I felt he was about to disclose something he believed in much more passionately than mathematics.

"The Liberal and Country Parties believe in the rights of the individual. They are opposed to Communism and Socialism." I knew he was having a go at Dr. Evatt, but there seemed nothing I could do to stop him. I tried to think what Father would say.

"Who controls the Labor Party?" Mr. Stewart asked the class. I put up my hand while everyone else was still thinking. He waited for a while, probably tired of having to ask me all the time.

"All right, Lynne," he said at last with a sigh, "What do you think?"

"I don't know who controls them, Sir, but I know they want to improve things for poor people."

"Ah, we've got a little socialist in our midst!" he said with a mocking laugh.

I was angry with myself for letting him humiliate me, but I never seemed to be able to stop myself from getting into arguments. I pictured his flashy silver car parked on the school grounds. He knew nothing about poverty. I did—or so I thought. Although our family was not poor in the conventional sense, my father's attitude to money made it seem as though we were. I remember one night when he was in one of his moods.

"You add it up," Mother had said, trying to balance the weekly budget. She slid a sheet of paper across the table. "I've checked it over and over, and I still get the same answer." Father grabbed the sheet, mumbling. The scowl on his forehead meant trouble. Thank goodness it wasn't me that time.

"Well, your addition is OK, but are you sure you entered everything you spent this week?"

"Yes, I know I did," said Mother, close to tears.

"You're still sixpence out," shouted Father. "You've got to find it. Check your purse again."

Mother pulled out the worn money purse from her old black

handbag and spread all the coins on the table. She put them in small piles: two shillings, shillings, sixpences, threepences, pennies, ha'pennies, then counted them again.

"It's just the same," she said, her eyes lowered.

Looking at my parents from the corner of the room, I was filled with anger—both with Father and with the unjust political system that had caused Mother such pain over a missing sixpence.

A few nights later, the screech of a microphone was heard from the end of the street. "Testing one, two, three, four… testing, testing."

"It must be one of the local candidates," said Father. "I think I'll wander down and have a listen."

"Can I come too?" I asked. I had never seen a live politician. There had to be something special about them, they were so powerful. They would have to be tough, too—with all the horrible things they said to each other in parliament.

"No, you can't," said Mother. "You haven't done the dishes for a week."

"She can come with me," said Father, "and do the washing up when she gets back."

As we hurried down the street, I glanced at the various houses to see if anyone else was coming. I tried to guess how each of our neighbors would vote. There were two Catholic homes in the street. According to Father, they would vote Labor. Then I remembered Aunty Mabel's statement: "We vote Liberal because we own property." Only the Cartwright-Brownes were rich enough to be in that category. That left a lot of people I could not account for.

The grass footpath extended along the side wall of the corner store and along the side of the concrete slab under the shop's awning, which faced onto the main road. I saw a truck parked diagonally on a broad strip of gravel between the front of the slab and the road. It looked like the sort of vehicle used to transport bales of hay. Bits of paint had been chipped off the panel work, and a section of the running board was missing. A huge Labor 'how to vote' sign—even larger than the posters on the telegraph poles—sat on the cabin roof.

On the back of the truck a tall, rugged-looking man had his hand over the microphone and was speaking to someone in the front. The fact that they could hear each other through the rectangle in the back wall of the cabin meant that the usual pane of glass was missing. Two old wooden chairs were placed between the microphone and the cabin. They reminded me of the creaky ones kept under the platform in our church hall.

Several people were standing near the truck on the footpath. I wondered if the candidate had brought them with him, as they were not from our area. Father took up a position underneath the shop awning. Perhaps he didn't want the neighbors to think he was part of the official group.

"Could you give us a hand up, mate?" A short man was trying to lift his right leg to the floor of the truck. It reached no higher than the rear number plate. The tall man leant down with one arm out, while a few men from the group on the footpath pushed the short man upwards, and he landed with a thud on the dusty floorboards. As he stood up, I recognized the face of Mr. O'Brien.

After brushing himself down, he moved towards a chair and pulled out some notes from inside his jacket. As he read them through quietly, he nodded his head and occasionally moved his hand in the air as though emphasizing a point. A wind had sprung up, blowing his straggly brown hair across his forehead. He looked up and grinned.

"Righto, mate, let's give it a go." The candidate folded his notes and placed them back in his jacket. The tall man cleared his throat and bent down to the microphone.

"Ladies and gentlemen, good evening. May I introduce the Labor candidate, Mick O'Brien."

"Hear, hear," said the men near the truck. I felt like joining in, but as Father did not, I kept quiet.

"The Australian Labor Party represents the only hope for justice in this country," he began. His voice was strong, and he spoke with passion and conviction. He said things that I had always believed, and I felt I could trust him. He looked earnestly into our faces. I looked back at him, hoping he would sense I was on his side. He quoted from Dr. Evatt's policy speech—increased medical and hospital benefits, equal pay for equal work, abolition of the means test for age pensions, more money to the States for housing.

By this time, a crowd had gathered in front of the shop. They listened quietly through the list of promised benefits. I felt the speech was going well. Surely any reasonable person would be impressed.

"Don't say anything!" a female voice behind me whispered.

"And let them get away with it?" an irate male voice responded.

"It's a blue-ribbon Liberal seat," the woman insisted. "This chap hasn't got a chance." The man grunted. Father half turned his head towards them. I was afraid he was going to start an argument.

"What about the Communists in the trade unions?" the man yelled.

"Edward, stop it!" the woman whispered, this time a bit louder. I was amazed that she had the courage to stand up to her husband, particularly in public. Sneaking a look around, I saw that the woman was about Mother's age.

"I'm glad you asked that question," said Mr. O'Brien calmly. "I'm actually a union secretary. I've never been a Communist, there are none in our union, and I don't even know any." I was so proud of his reply; I felt like cheering.

"That's a laugh," said the man. "How about your leader? He was legal counsel for the Communist Party in the High Court!"

"A barrister can represent any type of client," said the candidate. "Dr. Evatt has pledged that a Labor government will support the Royal Commission Mr. Menzies has set up to investigate espionage…"

"They won't have to look too far!" the man interrupted.

"Let the candidate continue his speech," snapped Father, swinging around and glaring at the man. I was pleased Father had stood up for Mr. O'Brien, but I wished someone else in the crowd could have done it. Now the neighbors would know how our family voted. The man behind made a threatening noise, and I was afraid of what Father might do. I had never seen him being attacked by someone his equal. With a complete stranger, he would not be able to use his usual line, "the subject's closed."

"It's all right," said the candidate in a reassuring manner. Although he must have been used to that type of interjection, I admired his composure. "We need to listen to all points of view."

At that moment, a huge gust of wind lifted the sign off the truck roof and hurled it against the Peters' ice cream advertisement on the front of the shop's awning. The sign fell in pieces onto the gravel.

"That's what'll happen to you lot in the election," said the interjector as he pulled his wife's arm and strode away. I looked up sympathetically at Mr. O'Brien as he glanced down at the remains of his sign. If he was upset, he did not show it.

A few other people left—I assumed they were Liberal voters—but the majority stayed. The fragments of the sign were picked up and placed on the floor of the truck.

"I think you all know my name by now anyway," he said with an embarrassed smile. "They regard this as a safe Liberal seat," he continued, "but a vote for Labor will send a message to Mr. Menzies."

At the end of the speech Father led some vigorous clapping. I joined in, though my hands were so small, they couldn't make much noise.

As the candidate was helped down from the truck, Father went over and pushed in front of everyone else.

"Congratulations on an excellent speech," he said, shaking the candidate's hand firmly. Before Mr. O'Brien could reply, Father put a hand on his upper arm and moved him away from the group. Mr. O'Brien looked back and winked at his supporters. I crept up as close as I could to hear what they were saying.

"I'm in great demand as a public speaker," said Father, "and I thought I could give you a few tips."

Again without waiting for a response, Father outlined his ideas on gestures and hand movements. He placed his arms in various positions, and he seemed to want Mr. O'Brien to copy him. But the candidate just nodded, occasionally sneaking a look back at his friends who were nudging each other at the impromptu oratory lesson. I felt Mr. O'Brien's gestures had been appropriate, but Father had a need to be copied by others. If they did not take his advice, he considered them incompetent.

"Thank you for taking the time to speak to me," said Mr. O'Brien, "but I should see a few other people before they leave." He moved away, leaving Father alone on the gravel. I was too embarrassed to move towards him—in fact, I did not even want to be seen with him. I thought of all his claims to Christian humility. How empty they seemed now.

"Some people have suggested I should go into politics," he said as we walked back up the street. "I know I'd do a great job, but I have been called to higher things."

I wondered whether this 'calling' included being a father, and what God thought of his efforts in that area. But I was beginning to think the two of them had similar ideas on the subject.

At home, I discovered to my relief that Mother had done the washing up, and she was in my bedroom, cleaning out a cupboard.

"How was it?" she asked in a dull voice.

"The man was very good," I said. "You might even have liked it."

"I don't think so," said Mother, as she firmly closed the cupboard door. "I don't believe in party politics. Everyone in parliament should be an Independent."

"But we never have an Independent standing in our electorate," I said, "so how do you vote?"

"I choose the candidate on the basis of his character."

"But how do you know what that is?" I asked, barely concealing my frustration.

"You can tell a man's character by his face," she declared.

I couldn't understand why Mother wouldn't tell me how she voted. Father made all the decisions for the family. She didn't even have to bother thinking about politics.

"Mother," I said emphatically, "which of the two parties has the candidates with the best faces?"

She waited a moment, then looked away. "The Liberal Party," she said.

My support for the Labor Party was undoubtedly based on their claim to work for the oppressed—in particular, those who had been born into circumstances from which they could not escape. Although our family was fairly secure financially, my father's punitive behavior had placed me in a position where I, too, felt trapped in a cage of ruthless oppression.

When I thought back on Father's engagement with the political candidate, I realized how inadequate he was and how insensitive and inappropriate his comments had been. He seemed to be oblivious to the attitudes of people around him. In some ways, this was a reflection of how he related to me. What I felt when he was using the cane on my flesh was a matter of complete indifference to him.

CHAPTER 13

New Adventures
on the Piano

"A child's return to Central, please." I pushed a shilling under the iron grill, and a ticket appeared beneath long, hairy fingers. It was three-thirty on a Monday afternoon, and the sun was scorching. The old corrugated iron roof of the station, which fulfilled its task protecting passengers from rain, gave up the struggle when confronted by that fiercer enemy. The waiting room furnace was deserted.

Walking over to the edge of the platform, I looked down at the four gleaming metal strips resting parallel on their somber supports and followed the two closest ones along the direction from which the train would come. The nearby level crossing was unprotected. Red and white lights at the side of the road had often proved inadequate for unwary motorists, whose fragile cages crumpled like toys before the ruthless onslaught of the iron juggernaut. A large bell and a red flag were carried along the track by a black-vested employee of Queensland Railways. He stopped where the barriers should have been, raising and lowering his arms with increasing urgency, perhaps wishing that he could convert himself, just for a few minutes, into a wooden beam with flashing lights.

A piercing hoot clashed with the sound of the bell, and an extra puff of smoke joined the streak of upward-floating pollutant, pretending to disappear into the atmosphere as though it had never existed. Another hoot as the sounds of wheel clatter grew, and the hissing, belching monster with its single eye, looked at a thirteen-year-old girl with the contempt it showed to all obstructions on its never-changing path.

I shrank back from the intensity, almost falling over, glimpsing an open fire and blackened engine hands. Hell was an eternal fire, some people said. Or was it just a symbol of punishment? In any case I wasn't going there. Father said he had to belt the devil out of me so I could go to Heaven. Surely, I had received enough of that to satisfy God.

The wheels screeched, and the passengers' heads jerked backwards or forwards, depending on their position in the carriage. I opened the door of the nearest compartment. The shutter had jammed halfway up. As I banged the door closed, the shutter fell out of sight, except for the groove in the top. After dusting soot from the seat, I sat on it and found myself opposite an opened newspaper. Parts of a hand could be seen on either side. On top was a forehead of crevices and clumps of limp hair. The paper dropped suddenly for thick-spectacled eyes to view the changing scenery. Then the face hid again.

My only trips to the city were to the dentist. Would this journey be as painful?

"You are going to a new piano teacher," Father had announced one night.

Miss Armstrong had gently guided me through the lower grades, but an "informed person" had suggested the change. My opinion on the matter was, of course, irrelevant.

The train entered Central tunnel, and the air in the carriage thickened. A few people began to cough as the lights dimmed, unable to compete with the sooty greyness. At length, the train arrived at Central Station. Small squares had been cut through the dark dome, suggesting contact with the outside world—an exchange of soot for car fumes.

After walking down Edward Street and along Queen Street, I arrived at King House, a center of excellence in music, with its brightly-lit store at street level. I pressed my nose against the window to look at all the shiny instruments. To the left of the store was the internal passageway. It began in light, but deeper into the building, it ended in gloom. My pace slowed as my eyes adjusted their focus. A horrible smell came from the darkness. I would not have been surprised to see a rat or two emerge. "This place gives me the creeps," I said out loud, half expecting to hear an echo.

Open iron railings formed the lift well. I pressed the brass button and waited. Nothing happened. I could just see the bottom of the lift opposite the first floor. Why wasn't it moving? I pressed the button harder, but there was no response. What kind of a building was this? And what strange people were its tenants? Mysteriously the lift then descended, creaking and groaning. Would I risk it? Well, at least it had a light that was working.

The journey began with a shudder. Halfway between the second and third floors the lift stopped. I pressed every button. "Move!" I shouted, banging my fist against the panel. I could not be late for my first lesson. I jumped up and down, wondering whether I should scream through the bars for help.

Suddenly there was a lurch. The lift went up, then down, then up again. It faced a dilemma. Would it convey the student to that strange place on the top floor? Nothing happened for several minutes. Then with a violent shudder, it shouted its warning and sped down to the ground floor.

I had a strong desire to walk straight out of the building, never to return. But what sort of reception would I get at home? The cane, of course. It was not worth it. My new teacher could not be as bad as that. I dragged both doors open, stepped out, then carefully closed them behind me before groping my way up four gloomy flights to the top floor. I stopped to get some breath. A dim light flickered, and there it was! A modest sign in gold print—"Vera Grant, FTCL."

Miss Grant's door was covered with a dark green felt layer for soundproofing. But where was I supposed to knock? I noticed a small window pane and raised my arm. Just in time, I heard the sound of a piano. Mother said it was rude to interrupt people. I waited for silence, then gently tapped my knuckles on the window, hoping my new teacher would be nothing like Father or Mr. Stewart.

The door opened, and an elderly, stout lady gave me a withering look. Her cold eyes looked in different directions, and a few streaks of brown dye in her hair made a sad contrast with the sea of surrounding grey. She attempted a smile. "You must be Lynne. Come in and sit over there, see?" What was I supposed to see? The lady was quite odd. And the room! The only window looked out onto a small gap between two grimy buildings. Inside it was musty and oppressive. The light was dull, and the ornaments on the mantelpiece looked as though they'd been there for fifty years. I felt I wanted to cut a huge hole in the ceiling to let in some sunlight and fresh air. Even a few drops of rain would have relieved the gloom.

The couch I had to sit on was all sag, no springs, as the student's lesson went on and on. Had the strange lady forgotten I was there? One good thing—she was obviously generous with her time. The student eventually departed, and I was invited to the piano.

"Well, what are you going to play for me?" I produced a fourth-grade piece and played it with a confidence I did not feel.

"I see," said Miss Grant. What did she see? Was my playing really so bad? Such a hard face. Surely her students were not her enemies?

I played some scales. "We've got a few things to fix up here," she said in a deep, scratchy voice. My hand position was corrected, my elbows were steadied, and my thumb was made to move more smoothly. Yes, Miss Grant was an expert. If only she were a bit more human.

On my arrival home, I had to face Father's interrogation.

"Well, how did it go? I hope you were courteous and didn't argue." Father had a habit of expecting the worst.

"Miss Grant seems to know more than Miss Armstrong. And I did behave properly."

"I'm pleased to hear it. Aunty Edna and the family are coming over tonight, and you will play a few pieces for them."

I dreaded playing in front of people. Even when I was practicing, a wrong note caused a sense of failure, but my sense of shame was overwhelming when other people were listening.

"I don't want to," I said. "In any case, they wouldn't be interested."

"You'll do as you're told, or I'll belt you." He stood up and moved towards me.

The pain Father inflicted on my body was one thing, but he would never understand the pain in my soul—the conflict between my need to believe that he did proclaim God's judgments, and my feeling that he was wrong—about me and perhaps about God as well. He saw me as evil. I saw myself as sensitive and kind. He confused me as to who I really was.

I thought of the way I wanted him to treat me. He could have said, "I understand how difficult it is for you to perform in front of people, but I would appreciate it if you could make the effort." With that conciliatory attitude, the hostilities would cease. We didn't have to be enemies. He must have believed that demonstrations of power would gain my respect. However, his misuse of that power had not only destroyed part of my soul, but it had ensured that one day I would reject him—forever.

CHAPTER 14

A Taste of Triumph

I wandered down the far end of the platform at Central, my eyes smarting from the cigarette smoke that rose above lines of black and grey suits. Dropping my music case to the ground, I put my head out through the iron railings, took some deep breaths, then turned around to face the empty section of the platform.

"I want you to work on a new piece," Miss Grant had said earlier that afternoon as she handed me the book of J.S. Bach's Two-part Inventions. "It's this one in B flat major." Opening my music case, I saw the face of the composer sketched on the cover of the book. He was middle-aged, with a sturdy, broad face, and there was an aura of serenity in his dark eyes.

The steam engine chugged slowly by, dragging its seven empty boxes. Before it came to a halt, hands grabbed for handles as work-weary bodies prepared to enter the compartments like self-stacking matchsticks. Running up to the end carriage, I stood at an open door and looked at the remaining few inches of floor space. "Just one more—only a small one?" I pleaded. The bodies took in a collective breath and shuffled backwards.

Pressing my case into my stomach, I climbed in sideways and pulled the door against me. At each station, I hopped out, then back in, till the friendly sign of the Walka Station released me from the cycle.

I led the way through the barrier, but I was soon outpaced by longer strides. Halfway up the steep hill, I stopped and peered down at the suburbs in the valley. Late afternoon clouds were hiding the setting sun. *If we lived there,* I thought, *I would be home by now, without aching legs. Why can't they have a bus service up the hill? But perhaps the engine wouldn't make it to the top. Only mountain goats belong in this terrain.* My breathing quickened as the angle of inclination increased. Our front gate seemed like the finishing line in an endurance trial. I leant on it and half ran, half fell, down the sloping path.

Ignoring weariness, I went straight to the piano. Deborah and Ruth left the room, but Jennifer stayed. She was the most musical member of the family and loved to listen to me play—even when I was struggling to learn something new.

What was this Bach and his "Invention" all about? I made an attempt at the piece, but it sounded like a lot of exercises joined together. *Oh well, I could hardly expect anything as good as Mozart.*

I practiced every day of the week, every week of the year. The only exception to this rule was Sundays. That was the "Lord's Day," Father said. I was only allowed to play hymns then. I pressed on with the piece until one morning, a few weeks later, something changed. Out of the mass of notes emerged a form—strong, yet gentle and beautiful. I was falling in love—not with a man, but with his exquisitely-structured music. I played the Invention over and over, each time becoming more enchanted with the rich harmonic intricacies of the weaving parts. As I closed the book, I looked again at the sketch on the cover. Those dark eyes seemed more intense; they must have touched the soul of the universe. I could hardly wait for my next lesson.

"Miss Grant," I asked, having no doubt about the answer, "who do you think is the greatest of all the composers?"

"I consider Beethoven is," she replied. This did not make sense. I had played a Beethoven piece before, but it was nothing compared to Bach.

"Do all musicians agree with this?"

"Oh no. Some would prefer Handel or Mozart, or Brahms. Some even Wagner."

"But what about Bach?" Miss Grant just had to like him. I looked at the wrinkles in her tight, drawn face. So much pain there. Had she ever really loved?

Miss Grant managed a half-smile. "Ah yes. I can see the effect the great composer has had on you."

"So other people like him as well?" The pitch in my voice rose as the tempo increased.

"Oh, yes. Many do. I just happen to prefer Beethoven." My face fell. I longed to share my new passion with my teacher. Did it take a special kind of intellect to plumb the depths of ultimate musical genius? Otherwise, how could anyone prefer any other composer?

I wondered if this was the closest to love I would ever be—with a man who had died in 1750. What was it that drew from me such a deep response? Would someone I loved have to be a musician? No. I could love a great scientist, a great painter—any kind of greatness that took a man beyond himself to the Source of knowledge itself.

"I think you're ready to do an exam," said Miss Grant at the end of an extended lesson.

"Can I play the Bach?" I asked eagerly.

"Certainly. It will be one of your four main pieces. Then there's an "extra list." The examiner usually only asks you to play one of them. And then there are scales and arpeggios, sight-reading, aural tests, and general knowledge."

"I'll work hard on all of them. It's funny, I hate playing in public, but when I do an examination, I get the feeling the examiner really wants me to do well. Then I play my best."

"A lot of students are the other way round. But I'm glad you like exams."

The much prepared-for day arrived. I put an arm out from under the mosquito net and reached for the clock. It was only 5.30. *I'll never get back to sleep* I thought, *but I can't practice my pieces because I'd wake Father and probably the neighbors as well. I'll just wriggle my fingers to get them supple.*

I looked across at Deborah breathing heavily under the blankets. The poor girl. She'd had her tonsils out and operations on her adenoids. But she often snored, and I hated having to drag my bedclothes out into the lounge whenever the noise woke me up.

"She's such a gentle girl," I said to myself. "Nothing like me. She never seems to get angry. How can she tolerate Father? At least I'm only punished when I've been arguing or lost something. But last night…"

"You've got these sums wrong," Father had shouted at Deborah, sitting opposite him at the table. Then he banged her across the head.

I watched in horror. I would love to have protected my sister, but my intervention would have worsened things. If only I had been a boy, and a bit older, I could have taken Father on. "You ever touch my sister again and I'll punch you." That would have fixed him, or would it?

Deborah never spoke about Father's cruelty. It seemed to me that she was like Mother—believing that suffering was part of life. Perhaps this was why Deborah eventually became a nurse—to help those in need. Years later, when she had completed her general training, she became interested in people with psychological problems, so she undertook studies in that area as well. Until her retirement, Deborah gave everything of herself in treating clients from difficult backgrounds who were barely coping with the challenges life presents.

I heard Father go into the bathroom. At last I could make some noise. I leapt out of bed, grabbed a dressing gown and raced to the piano. It was a cold morning, but my body was hot. My fingers flew across the keyboard.

"I don't feel like breakfast," I said to Mother. "My tummy's all churned up."

"It'll be even more churned up in the middle of the exam if you don't eat. You need Vitamin B."

Mother poured wheatgerm into my bowl and lifted my hand onto the milk jug.

Fortified with Mother's breakfast, I walked briskly to the station, passing the more relaxed office workers who knew, from the sound of the train in the distance, that it would arrive in exactly two and a half minutes. I checked the contents of my music case several times—a note to my form master, explaining my absence, a list of pieces to give the examiner, and all my music books. *I know it's all there,* I thought, shaking my head, *but I have to keep checking.*

I was offered a few inches on the edge of a seat in the crowded train. I accepted it as a compliment, but my small knees were buffeted with the build-up of human cargo. Then a jerky bus ride provided a different kind of test for my fingers as I hung on grimly to the straps.

The long, narrow windows of the imposing examination building were slightly open. I put a hand behind my ear but could not hear a sound. Inside, the musty smell of an old red carpet and high, dark walls made me feel like an unwelcome stranger. I walked up the stairs to a bleak waiting room, where everyone spoke in whispers, as though it were a funeral parlor.

The supervisor, who looked as cold as the room, took my identification sheet. She read it through then looked at me without any change in facial expression. "That seems to be correct," she said.

Miss Grant sat in a far corner of the room, looking more somber than usual. "I didn't know you were going to be here," I said, taking a seat beside her.

"I always come to hear my students play," a sad voice replied.

"That must be a real ordeal for you, having to listen to all of us. Can you hear everything from out here?"

"Unfortunately, yes," she said, wincing as the sound of a wrong note came through the examination room door. "I usually feel sick the whole time." I felt like patting her arm, but I was unsure what the response would be as I had never touched her before. Despite her strange manner, Miss Grant was an amazing person.

The door opened, and a young girl in a white dress emerged. Her eyes were red, and she was holding a crumpled handkerchief. "I won't be like that at the end of my exam," I said to Miss Grant, "unless, of course, the examiner's a monster."

"You can go in now." The supervisor mouthed the words, with barely a sound escaping her lips.

Miss Grant and I exchanged reassuring glances as I tiptoed in to the examination room. The sun was streaming in through a high window onto the desk where the examiner was busily writing. She looked up and smiled, her soft green eyes reaching out in welcome. We chatted for a few minutes, and to my surprise, I found myself relaxing.

"Could you play me the scale of D major?" asked the examiner in a voice so gentle she could have been hushing a baby to sleep. The easy opening scale was followed by some harder ones. I was not afraid of any of them; I had practiced them all so many times.

The piano's tones were richer than I was used to, and my first piece sounded even better to my ears. Then I lifted the book of Two Part Inventions onto the music rack. The great composer had become my friend. I looked into his eyes again, and it felt like our souls had become one. As I began to play the piece, I felt I was being taken over by a greatness I could not understand. At the end, I looked across at the examiner, who seemed to be in a trance.

After such an experience, I felt that nothing could go wrong, but soon came the moment I had been dreading. The examiner placed a piece of music in front of me. It was the sight-reading test.

I thought of my previous exam when, in my impatience, I had begun playing the piece without looking at the key signature. At the end of the first line, I realized something was wrong. Without asking the examiner—a man on that occasion—I played the piece again, this time with the two required flats, but at such a speed, my fingers fell over each other. It was humiliating to think about it. I would not make that mistake now.

"Take your time," said a calm voice. How could the lovely examiner know that I needed such a warning? I looked at the piece. It had only one sharp and was just crotchets and quavers. This was too good to be true. I felt the examiner must have taken a liking to me for some inexplicable reason, as I played the piece like an expert.

"We'll do the aural tests now." She sat at the piano, and I removed myself the required distance. The lovely lady's face beamed each time I gave the correct answer. She was an angel.

By the end of the examination, I felt as though I was floating. I was determined to have this experience again and again. If only

I could get the beautiful lady each time! We said goodbye, and I hurried through the door to find out my teacher's reaction.

The smile on my face disappeared as I looked across the room. The creases in that worn forehead had become furrows. Had the performance made her ill? Were there some wrong notes? Miss Grant looked up, and a light from an unknown source seemed to erase the lines of care.

"You did very well," she whispered. I let out a huge sigh, then quickly put my hand over my mouth. The supervisor glared. I apologized, mimicking the lady's voiceless lips.

"Thank you for everything, Miss Grant," I said in subdued excitement as I tiptoed out of the room.

I raced down the stairs, singing at the top of my voice. I didn't care about the supervisor. And I even forgot about Father. Perhaps God had felt sorry for me and had given me a break. Whatever it was, I would try to remember that everything was on my side, at least for one glorious day.

Having got something right gave me a sense of joy that I had often sensed in some believers. I assumed this was caused by the relationship they had with God, and that their joy could never be extinguished by adversities in their lives. By contrast, my sense of elation could only ever be temporary since I felt like a failure in all my attempts to establish a relationship with my Creator.

CHAPTER 15

My Ticket to Acceptance

In the eyes of my parents, I did not measure up. I was supposed to conform to the image of a female presented in the Bible, but because of my nature, I was incapable of meeting this demand. My parents' reactions to me ranged from deep disappointment to a belief that they could somehow force me to become meek, quiet, and acquiescent by inflicting physical pain. The only part of me they could accept was that I was conscientious in whatever I did. This included my dedication to music. If I could keep on achieving in this area, perhaps their attention would be directed away from my failure as a female to my success as a human being.

"They're looking for new choir members," said our musical next-door neighbor. "Why don't you have a go?"

"But wouldn't I have to pass an audition?"

"Yes, but you're a musician. You'll be fine." But I had doubts about that since my singing voice sounded like a frog with bronchitis.

I remembered the first time I heard the Queensland State and Municipal Choir.

"What's that lovely music?" I asked.

"It's Handel's 'Messiah.'" Father monitored the family radio. Only religious programs were allowed on Sundays. No sport—not even the news. On other days, the programs had to be appropriate for a Christian household. Handel's music passed the test.

I thought of our local church choir. The sopranos wobbled, the tenors screeched, and the basses were behind the beat. But this choir was different. How I would love to sing under a great conductor. But what if I failed the test?

The City Hall. Massive Greek columns. World-famous artists. Thunderous applause. Burial ground for failures. I looked at the awesome building near the fountain in St. George's Square. Its great tower surveyed the city like an ancient king in his kingdom. The giant white clock struck six, obliterating the sounds of sirens, bells, and motors. All around the square, the pigeons, having feasted on afternoon scraps, were cooing their thanks. What unchallenged lives they led. No one tested *their* ability to create a pure tone. Could I bear it if my vocal cords were found wanting?

Slowly I walked up the broad stairway and stopped beside a column. There was still time to go home. No one would ever know. But could I live with myself if I acted like a coward? My heart was pounding as I approached the audition room at the end of the corridor. The sound of a silvery tenor floated through the door. I thought of my own meagre vocal capacities. My throat began to dry, and then it tightened. The door opened, and the proud tenor walked briskly out. What was I doing there? I must have lost my senses.

"I'm so pleased you've come." Alfred Grice, the conductor, smiled at me. "This won't be painful at all." How could he tell I wanted to flee? He gave me a music sheet, but my shaking hands made it difficult for my eyes to focus. Mr. Grice played the first note. I opened my mouth, but nothing came out.

"Let's have another go." I just had to relax my throat muscles. A further attempt, but again no sound. Why had I put myself through this hell?

"One more time." A few croaky notes. My throat was choking. I submitted to fate.

"I'm so terribly sorry," I said, turning to leave the room. The gracious man looked at me with his kind eyes.

"You're one of Miss Grant's students, aren't you?"

"Yes," I said breathlessly. *What was this all about? How did he know? And what difference did it make?*

"I think we could have you in the choir."

"You mean I've passed?" It wasn't possible. It was a miracle!

"Thank you, thank you so much, Mr. Grice." The words gushed out. "I haven't got much of a voice, but I will work terribly hard."

"I know you will," he said.

That wonderful man had done something I had never experienced before. He had put his faith in me against the overwhelming evidence of my inadequacy. I resolved that I would never let him down.

The uniform for the ladies in the choir was a long white gown. I stood on the kitchen table as Mother adjusted the hemline of my first full-length dress. *What a terrible existence she has*, I thought. *The sewing machine, the washing machine, the stove. No life of her own. Humiliated by the man she married and a slave to her children.*

Accepting Mother's hand, I lowered a foot to the chair. That rough, weather-beaten skin. What was it like when she was young and free? So talented, she could have done anything. So lovely she could have married anyone.

Murray Walters was a former suitor whom Mother had never forgotten. He belonged to the "high church" branch of the Church of England. Mother went to the Gospel Hall. They fell in love, and tried each other's churches. "I knew he was a believer," she said, "he was so devout. But those prayers to saints—and 'offering up Christ' at the communion service. It was so wrong."

"And what did he think of your church?"

"He couldn't believe he was actually in church. Couldn't stand it."

"So what happened?"

"Eventually, we broke up. The pain…" I looked into Mother's sad eyes. She deserved better than this. If only she'd married Murray, I would have been a different person. Sweet and gentle. None of those rotten Lewis genes. Perhaps such a father would have loved me almost as much as he loved Mother.

The upbringing my mother had to endure was probably even worse than that of my father. Her own father died of war injuries when she was very young and her mother had serious financial difficulties. She tried to survive by investing in a small shop, but since hardly anyone at that time had the ability to pay her, she became insolvent. Rather than going through the humiliation of bankruptcy, she worked long hours into the night for many years, making dresses for customers, until she had paid off the last of her debts. My mother, however, told me she only ever had two dresses.

I surveyed the gown Mother had made for me in one of our long mirrors. It was fitting for the City Hall stage, and I looked older than my sixteen years. "Thank you so much," I said, flinging my arms around Mother. But she could not respond.

It was the night of the concert. I arrived early and walked up the wide marble stairway to the gallery. As a child, I had played hide-and-seek there with my sisters. I loved the feel of the smooth, shapely cream balusters and the broad, shiny slab on top.

The concert hall structure was a circle, and everything in the building conformed to a circular pattern—stage, gallery, and choir stalls. The roof formed a cream dome, with a golden circle at the base. The light seemed to reach down from heavenly spheres, drawing everything back to it in a joyful embrace. I would soon be singing of the loving Father who dwelt above the stars and set them on

LEAVING FAITH, FINDING MEANING

their courses—the Ode to Joy, immortalized in Beethoven's Ninth Symphony.

The gallery and the main hall began to fill with music-lovers, subscribers, and choir members' friends and families. I floated down the steps, along the corridor and into the assembly room, amid a sea of white gowns. *Was I really here—with this choir of angels?*

At the appointed time, the choristers moved with dignity across the stage to the choir stalls, carrying their music in the prescribed manner. The overhead lights were dazzling. I blinked and lowered my eyes. Members of the symphony orchestra wandered in, adjusted their seats and music stands, and began to tune up. I was almost on top of them. So much better than my usual position—in the cheap seats at the back of the hall.

The visiting conductor made his entrance, and the choir and the orchestra stood. After the customary acknowledgements, the choir sat, and the performance began. I looked at the conductor, then at the instrumentalists. Unlike choristers, they didn't seem to look at him very often. Perhaps as professional musicians, they didn't need to. The third movement ended, and the choir stood.

My heart was pounding. It wasn't an audition, and I wasn't playing in public. What was I scared of? If I sang, I might spoil it. I would just open my mouth and pretend. But rich contralto sounds engulfed me. I wanted to be a part of it—to add my small contribution to the great chorus. Mesmerized by the conductor, I forgot the printed page, pouring out my heart and soul in the Song of Joy.

The audience exploded. The conductor and soloists bowed, and the orchestra was acknowledged. Then a black-coated arm pointed to the choir. "Bravo!" The cries rang out from the audience above the applause. People stood in their seats. I longed to acknowledge it—to wave, or bow, or smile. The conductor and soloists returned to the stage again and again. Would the applause ever cease?

There was no one at the City Hall to tell me I had done well that day. But it didn't matter. I was part of a triumph. Did I really need the approval of anyone? Joy was at the heart of the universe, and the loving Father wanted me to be happy. This was such a rare experience that I clung to those feelings for as long as I could.

CHAPTER 16

Forbidden to Be a Teacher

"God is our refuge and strength." Non-reflecting glass covered the text on the cream painted wall above the piano. The words sat easily, surrounded by a floral border. When thundered by a preacher with university degrees they even sounded convincing. *But where was God,* I thought, *when Father reached for the cane?* That exalted Being was not my refuge. He was nowhere to be found. According to Father, God had dictated every word in the Bible, which told him he had to bring his children up "in the discipline of the Lord." Therefore, he saw beating his eldest daughter as the work of God. So the Being was there, after all, causing pain to my body.

Was it worth believing in this kind of God? The Bible said a non-believer would suffer in Hell forever. One lifetime's sins and the offender were punished for billions of years. That kind of justice would hardly be worthy of a corrupt dictator. I lowered my eyes from the text to my new piece open on the music rack. Chopin's Revolutionary Study. So many revolutions in human history. Innocent people slaughtered. Why should I expect to escape injustice?

"This piece is to strengthen your left hand," Miss Grant had said. It looked horribly difficult. I was relieved it was only an exercise.

The piano was against the wall dividing the lounge from the kitchen. As I advanced in my music studies, the volume of sound echoing through the wall increased.

"That noise is going right through my head," Mother complained. Even with the door closed, her hearing aid distorted the sound.

"I'll cover the strings inside the piano with a sheet, so the hammers will only produce a dull thud." I rummaged through the linen cupboard's bottom shelf and found an old sheet covered with scorch marks. Then I jammed it at either end of the piano lid hinge and let it fall over the strings. The noise level was greatly reduced, but the action of the keys did not feel right to my fingers.

"I'm sorry, Mother," I said. "It won't work."

"Well, you'll just have to cut down on your hours of practice."

"That's impossible!" I said. "You're always telling us that it's not worth doing anything unless you can do it well."

"But other students don't drive their families mad the way you do."

"They don't have to work as hard. They're more musical than I am and their hands are stronger."

"It's no good trying to reason with you. You're just so pig-headed."

Mother walked out of the room. I knew she hated arguments, but the present problems I regarded as her fault. It had all begun with a conflict a few years earlier, which determined the course of my life.

"You're going to leave school at the end of the year," Father had declared.

"But I'm only sixteen. I want to finish high school and become a teacher."

"Definitely not," said Mother. "You're too aggressive already. No man will ever want you the way you are. And you're too intelligent for your own good. If a woman has brains, she must hide them. Being a teacher would just encourage you to air your opinions."

The family knew two single female teachers, delightful people brimming with confidence. Mother disliked the fact that they even extended a hand to shake hers! She was terrified I would finish up like them because of my unfortunate personality. The way she saw it, to produce a daughter who never married would have been a sign of failure on her part. It was her responsibility, or so she thought, to raise her daughter to conform to the New Testament view of a female who was quiet and submissive. Her rejection of my basic personality was probably even more detrimental to my self-esteem than my father's cruelty. At least with Father, I realized from the beginning that the way he punished me was outrageous, but when Mother described me, she seemed to have God on her side.

"You can get a job in an office," Father added. "In that kind of environment, you'll have to keep quiet and do as you're told."

"I see!" I glared at him. "In other words, you want me to become a nothing—perhaps lose the skill of being able to challenge you."

"Do you want a belting now?" said Father. The question ensured my silence.

"You don't have to become a nothing," said Mother. "You can concentrate on your music and do your letters."

"They're not called 'letters' Mother. It's a diploma."

"Oh well, whatever it's called. You know that all you girls have to qualify at something."

"Yes, I know that. But I have more intelligence than musical ability. Surely, God would want me to concentrate on the area where he has given me the skills."

"In the first Epistle of Peter," Father declared, "it says a woman must have a gentle and quiet spirit. That hardly describes you, does it?" Father looked at me with contempt. I held my body rigid: Father and God—a punitive combination. I had been cheated of the only career I had ever wanted—all because I had been born with the wrong kind of personality. It seemed so unfair when my parents later allowed my sister, Ruth, to become a teacher, her personal characteristics being acceptable to them. By contrast, I was condemned to spend years of drudgery in the Commonwealth Public Service. Entry required proficiency in typing and shorthand, so instead of being sent to a regular high school, my parents decided to enroll me in a commercial college. My first job required me to type out the questions people had missed on their pension application forms.

But outside office hours, my primary focus was on music. Day after day, for eighteen months, I battled with the Chopin. Eventually, it was note-perfect—but nothing more.

"Do you think my left hand is a bit stronger now?" I asked Miss Grant.

"Yes, it is," she said. "In fact, I want you to play this at my student recital."

I could not believe it! The piece was technically beyond me. My teacher had deceived me, and was now giving me an impossible burden.

"I can't do it, Miss Grant. After all this time, I still can't play it at the correct speed. It'd sound terrible."

"Of course, you can do it. You've got a few more months to work on it. It'll be all right."

From the tone in her voice, which at times reminded me of Father's, I realized the discussion had ended. Yet again, I thought, someone in authority is demanding that I do the impossible.

At 5.06 pm on the day of the recital, I removed my carefully-protected dress from a cupboard in the office. It was an embroidered light blue satin—one of Mother's special efforts. I folded it over my right arm, used my left hand to clock-off, then walked down the steps. I wouldn't risk getting the dress squashed in the rush-hour lift.

Tram after tram flashed its way across Victoria Bridge in a silver blur, long black rods drawing power from the lines above as the sparks showered. I watched motorists playing mind games with pedestrians, each claiming a prior right to the roadway between the footpath and the safety zone. To me, trams were cold, heartless things. I hated the constant stopping and starting and the struggle people had to get to the door. The drivers in their sealed-off boxes were protected from the sounds of irate passengers, when their inept handling of the controls threw the strap-hangers on top of each other. I tried to stroll along Queen Street, but I was soon pulled along by the rush-hour crowd.

The basement of the City Hall had a shower room for ladies. The smell of steam and perfumed soap welcomed me as I handed a sixpence to the attendant, whose straight grey hair was parted down the middle and dragged back behind her ears.

"Would you like a towel, love?" Her smile revealed crooked, blackened teeth.

Looking at the old lady, I was grateful to Mother for sending me to the South Brisbane Dental Hospital to have my teeth straightened. Beneath the shower, I felt a bond with all the other weary office workers as they washed away the reminders of their lowly status. Here they could come alive again, throw off their drab uniforms, and admire the reflection of their unacknowledged beauty.

I emerged from this process of transformation in the belief that Mother would consider my appearance "appropriate for the occasion." I would now practice an elegant walk along Adelaide Street in place of my usual ungainly dash. The peak hour scramble of bodies had given way to the more leisurely stroll of dinner suits and evening gowns. I felt at home in this company until I turned into Edward Street. On the edge of the footpath, a bedraggled man was leaning against the serving counter of a pie stall, a bottle of beer in one hand and a pie in the other. Should I join him to get a cheap meal? What would Mother say? I edged closer towards the fragile structure, looking around to make sure there was no one I knew who could report my inelegant choice. I stood at the opposite end of the pie stall from the only other patron, but the smell of alcohol almost obliterated the more wholesome aroma of meat and gravy, peas, and tomato sauce. The man behind the counter looked at my dress.

"You'd better not spill anything on that," he said, raising a finger in warning. He placed the pie on a tin plate, and I tilted my body forwards.

The venue for the recital was the Albert Hall, near King George Square. At 7 p.m. I walked up the steps to the foyer, where Mother was chatting with a group of ladies. In the perfumed air were gowns of shantung, brocade, and chiffon, a string of cultured pearls, a marcasite brooch, clutch bags, and stoles. A brown fur with a fox's head rested across a lady's shoulder. The dark, shiny eyes looked into mine. They belonged in the wild. Part of me belonged there too.

"Have you had dinner, dear?" Mother asked.

"Well… yes." I was frantic, trying to signal to Mother for the questioning to stop.

"Where did you go?" she asked, not reading my strange facial expressions.

"Oh, just down Edward Street."

"Are there any restaurants in that part of the city?" Mother was trying to picture the area.

"Well, no… I… um…" My fast-moving brain had never let me down before. *Please, please, mind, think of something. Rescue me!* But it had deserted me. I was alone.

"Well… I… I… went to a pie stall."

"You actually ate at a pie stall in your lovely dress!" Mother could not hide her embarrassment, shaking her head as she closed her eyes. The others laughed.

"I was careful," I said, still trying to think of an excuse.

"What a delightful daughter you have," said the lady with the fox's head. "She's such an original." My humiliation was complete.

The group accepted programs from a boy in a white shirt and bow tie, and walked down the auditorium aisle in a manner befitting ladies who do not frequent pie stalls.

Miss Grant wore a sequined floor-length pink gown. She sat to the left of the stage, just out of sight of the audience. Despite her attire, her facial expression displayed the kind of anguish she experienced every year, with her self-imposed ordeal in the music examination waiting room.

The first student ran up the steps, played a simple piece, took a brisk bow, turned, and ran down again. I was waiting for him in the shadows.

"That sounded lovely," I said. "I'm organizing a surprise presentation to Miss Grant. Would you like to make a contribution?"

"I'll ask Mum," he replied as I watched to see where 'Mum' was located. A similar request was made to each performer, and the donations flowed in.

Between my money-collecting activities, I walked up the steps to play my Chopin study. Having worked on it for two years, I did not need the music. But with the brilliant stage lights, the gleaming Steinway, and the sight of the audience out of the corner of my eye, I longed for the familiar sight of the well-worn pages.

The applause was generous, and I was relieved. Yet I had not measured up to my own standards. I could not play the Chopin the way the professionals did; it didn't sound "right." *What was I doing, pretending to be a pianist?*

The final student played a Beethoven sonata. I could hardly suppress the feelings of envy that flooded over me as I marveled at the brilliance of the player's technique.

"That was magnificent," I said as the talented girl reached the bottom of the stairs. "Would you be willing to make a presentation to Miss Grant on behalf of all her students?"

"I'd love to," she said, with the charm of an accomplished artist. "No one has ever done that for Miss Grant before." I handed her the huge sheaf of flowers I had bought for our teacher that day.

The star of the recital enticed Miss Grant out onto the stage. I moved back along the aisle to watch the presentation. The intensity of the applause convinced me, just for a moment, that Father was wrong. Despite everything he said about me, I was a good person.

I walked back to the foyer, where the ladies were making appropriate noises of commendation to Mother, who smiled in appreciation.

"I guess there are compensations for having a headstrong daughter," she said.

Overall, I felt the evening had been a success. But was it worth it? Two years' work—all over in a few minutes. Why did I drive myself so hard? And why couldn't I somehow be superhuman and do better than my best? For Mother and Father, my best each day was unacceptable—to them, and to God as well. If only I could be a better person, I would pass the test. But I had to find out what the test was all about or whether my personal inadequacies had destined me to be a never-ending failure.

CHAPTER 17

Learning the
Pipe Organ

*T*hank goodness I'll never have to ride in this wonky lift again.
I was visiting Miss Grant after my Trinity College Associate
diploma examination. It would not be an easy parting. The smell
of the old musty room greeted me for the last time as my teacher
opened her felt-covered door.

"You look happy enough," she said.

"Well, I enjoyed it. John Symons is a delightful English
gentleman. But the poor man was stuck somewhere out in the
country where he'd been examining, and he was two hours late.
Another girl and I had a long go on the piano. We were lucky the
supervisor was in a good mood."

"I was sorry I couldn't be there this time. How was your playing?"

"No wrong notes. But I thought I'd blown it in the teaching
section when he asked what Beethoven I would give a beginner. I
kept on saying 'Beethoven, Beethoven' as though I was calling up
his spirit. I don't know whether the great master heard me or not,
but I had a flash. 'Oh! I suppose he wrote some sonatinas.'"

"Just as well you thought of it."

"Yes, it was a near thing. The examiner seemed as relieved as I was.
The way he said 'Indeed, Beethoven *did* write some sonatinas'—there
was something in the tone of his voice. I felt I'd made it."

"I'm sure you have."

"Miss Grant, I want to thank you for all the help you have given me over so many years."

"You sound as though you're leaving me!"

I stared at her. "I thought you knew that."

"No, I didn't. I expected you to stay with me and do a Licentiate diploma. I think you owe me that."

I took a deep breath and looked up on top of the piano. Photographs of Miss Grant's Licentiate and Fellowship graduates were smiling at me. Yes, I owed her a debt of gratitude, but not another diploma. I didn't belong to that brilliant lot up there. At the age of twenty, I felt I had given everything I could to my piano studies.

"I think I've done enough exams. I don't want to be a piano teacher, and in any case, I don't have the technical ability to go any higher."

"So you're going to forget about music?"

"Oh no. I've been thinking for some time about learning an instrument that has always fascinated me—the pipe organ."

"I see. Well, I guess that's better than nothing. As a Bach lover, you should do well at it. Where will you go?"

"'I think I'll try Archie Day."

"Dear Archie." Miss Grant's voice was unusually tender. "You'll like him."

She stood abruptly and walked to the door, preparing to sever a bond with a student who had done her best—perhaps more than her best—with her limited ability. The two of us had not become friends, but there was deep respect between us.

"Good luck in whatever you do." I felt the pain in her voice. There was a pang in my own heart, too, as I said goodbye. I walked slowly out and heard the door click behind me. Perhaps Miss Grant would actually miss me. That thought had not occurred to me before. I always believed that even my own parents would be glad to get rid of me.

Later that day, I sat at the dining room table to compose a letter to Mr. Day. I thought of the strange things that had happened at that table. On Sundays at lunchtime, it was the scene of competition between our parents, though Mother would never have acknowledged that, even to herself. Each week she would seek out the lonely and the stranger at church and invite them home to lunch. On the previous Sunday, the guests had been an engineer and his wife from England. After an exchange of pleasantries, Mother asked about their children.

"We have a son and a daughter. They're both at university."

"Are they—"

"What do you think about the doctrine of divine election?" Father's booming voice obliterated the inquiry.

"Well… I think… perhaps… there are various ways of looking at it," said the engineer, looking helplessly at his wife.

"This is how I see it," said Father, as he began one of his endless monologues. I felt like crawling under the table as I looked at Mother's face. The light had gone out of her eyes, and I could almost hear an inward sigh. I would probably never marry, but I would not tolerate that kind of behavior from any man if I did. But then, what man other than Father would be like that?

I filled my fountain pen with Quink blue. Should I try to impress my prospective teacher—or perhaps he would require me to audition. A person of his status, who held the title of City Organist could afford to be choosy about students. I outlined my examination results for piano and the theory of music. In the latter, I had topped the State.

A few days after I posted the letter, the phone rang. "Mr. Day says he'll take me!" I called out, running through the house.

"Where do you have to go for lessons?" asked Deborah.

"Albert Street Methodist. It's the most beautiful church you could imagine."

The church stood tall like a stately lady with her narrow spire and her dress of rich red brick trimmed with squares of cream stone. She looked across to King George V, by the grace of God, Defender of the Faith, sitting in bronze upon his horse in the center of the Square that bore his name. Each Saturday afternoon, the church's bells pealed for couples who had pledged their love. It was a setting from which love seemed to flow. Steeply sloping galleries along three sides of the building created a feeling of intimacy. Organ pipes in blue and gold spread across the sanctuary wall. In front of the pipes were the choir stalls in a semi-circle, with the organ console in the center.

The side door was open as I arrived at the church for my first lesson. Soft music was playing, and I waited in a front pew. The sound seemed to come from another dimension, permeating every cell in my body. Tears filled my eyes as I allowed the music to embrace my innermost being. My mind went back to a service I had attended there a few years earlier.

What a contrast between that and our church at Walka. I was tired of hearing that people would go to Hell if they did not repent. There was nothing of that at this church. At Walka, I felt judged; here, I felt caressed. It was a different kind of God. I did not tell Mother and Father how I felt about that service. They had only grudgingly allowed me to go.

"We don't think the gospel is preached there," Mother had said. "These 'liberal' churches just talk about making the world a better place. They never address the real issue—human sinfulness." I hardly needed to go to church to hear about my sinfulness. At home, it was the main topic of conversation.

"Come on up." A bright, cheery voice broke the spell.

My new teacher had a lively face, a deep suntan and thick white hair. His movements were quick, and he spoke in short, clipped sentences.

"Slide along the organ stool. But don't tread on the pedals." I looked down and noticed that the pedals were in the same form as the notes on the keyboard, only much larger.

"Yes, they are all notes. They're kept highly polished. Your feet have to move across them easily. You will have to get special organ shoes. Don't wear them anywhere else. Dancing shoes are the best."

"All those stops! And three keyboards!" I smiled with delight.

"They're called manuals. The fundamental one, in the middle, is the Great. The one above is the Swell. The lower one is the Choir."

"What do you do with three manuals?"

"Each one has different tone qualities. It depends on the stops you select. These stops here, for example, relate to the Swell."

"How about the pedal notes. Do they have stops?"

"Yes, they're over here."

"And what are all those buttons just below the keys?"

"They're called pistons. Press one of them. See what happens."

I pressed piston 4, and an array of stops popped out.

"Now play a chord." I did so, and a majestic sound filled the building. A chill went up my spine.

"That is magnificent!" I could hardly believe I had created it.

"Organ playing has to be legato—smooth, connected. There's no sustaining pedal as there is on the piano. Decide what fingers to use to get a good legato and then write them down under each note."

The lesson went so smoothly and pleasantly, I could hardly believe it was a man who was teaching me. My experiences with male authority figures up until then had aroused only anger and fear. Mr. Day gave me hope that I could relate to a man without alienating him and that I could even enjoy the experience

At my first practice, I studied the exercises for the pedals. Different signs above or below the note indicated whether it would be played by the right toe, right heel, left toe or left heel. Positioning my body on the organ stool created a problem. If I sat comfortably, my legs could not reach both ends of the pedal board, but I was likely to fall off when I sat right on the edge of the seat.

"Well, how did it go?" Mother seemed delighted I was studying the organ. I would be of use in the church.

"It's terribly hard playing the pedal notes without looking at them. It's like learning to touch type, only when you get it wrong it's a horrible sound."

"But how do you find where the notes are?"

"Well, your toe has to feel for the gap between the groups of the three black notes and the two black notes. Except that on the pedal board they're not painted black. The worst thing is that you often miss a note and finish up pressing two together."

"You play the piano so well. I know you'll be brilliant on the organ. But it does seem a big instrument for such a little body."

Mother was so full of encouragement, even though she was not in the least musical. I thought perhaps that was a reason she wanted me to excel. But there was one good thing about learning the organ. Never again would Mother have to endure endless hours of reverberation through the lounge/kitchen wall.

CHAPTER 18

Life is So Unfair

"Now comes the hard part," said Mr. Day. "Organ music has three staves, two for your hands and the bottom one for your feet. The problem comes with your left hand. It's used to playing the lowest notes on the page, so it keeps trying to do so."

I was puzzled. If the left hand knew it had to play the middle stave, why would it want to do anything else?

"You don't believe me? Well, try this." Mr. Day produced a simple exercise in two staves.

"Now play the top one with your left hand and the bottom one with your feet."

"That looks like a Grade 1 piece!"

"Have a go." He gave me a knowing smile. The first note on each stave was a C. That was easy. The second note went up to a D for the left hand and down to a B for the feet.

"I can't believe this. My left hand refuses to play a D. It keeps going down to a B. I must be going crazy."

"No, you're not. You'll feel crazy for about six months. Then your brain will be reprogrammed."

I could understand why so many pianists discontinued their organ studies. But I was going to master it, no matter what.

A few days later, the phone rang at home.

"It's for you," said Father. "The Trinity College office."

My diploma examination had been several months ago, so

I wondered why they were ringing me now.

"Listen to this, everyone!" I called out, dropping the receiver. "I've topped the State in my piano diploma. They'll give me an award, but only if I play one of my exam pieces at a prize winners' concert in three weeks. I have to let them know."

"That would be a fitting reward for all your hard work."

Father's tone was unusually kind. The only time he seemed to appreciate me was when I had done something worthwhile. He liked that I would mow the front lawn and trim the edges without being asked. And that I helped him build the retaining wall for the bottom terrace and painted the outside of the house with him. He had built some sturdy scaffolding for that task, but the back of the house was so high, I was terrified to look down. My painting outfit was one of his old shirts that barely reached my thighs.

"You look like nothing on earth!" said Grandma Denham, who spent most days of the week helping Mother make our clothes.

"Nothing on earth, nothing in heaven, but something somewhere else," replied Father, in one of his rare playful moods.

The opportunity to perform at the concert caused me a problem. I had not touched the piano since the day I said goodbye to Miss Grant. Thinking that I would have no further use for my music, I had offered it to her, but she was so upset about my giving up the piano I eventually decided to keep it. I knew this would be the most critical audience I would face in my life. Because I had always hated performing, I usually managed to escape it, apart from the occasional Sunday School concert at which Father commanded me to play. This time, any wrong note would be a disaster. I thought about each of my pieces—*Bach, Haydn, Chopin. Which of them would hold together best under the stress of performance?* Within a few minutes, I was on the phone again.

"I will play at your concert. Bach's Prelude and Fugue in C Minor, Book 2."

"I thought I'd heard the last of that piece," said Mother in mock exasperation, as the familiar notes of the Prelude she had listened to for eighteen months once more resounded through the kitchen wall.

I rang Mr. Day to give him the news and to cancel the following three lessons. Organ and piano techniques were quite different. In any case, I wanted to devote every second to the perfect performance of my beloved Bach.

A fortnight later, the examination office rang again. At the end of the conversation, I slammed down the phone.

"Of all the stupid idiots! They tell me I cannot play the Bach piece a week before the performance. The Licentiate winner wants to play it, and, of course, she gets priority."

"Well, if anyone can do the impossible, you can." Mother could always lift my spirits.

It would have to be my Haydn sonata—more technically demanding than the Bach and only seven days to prepare it. I could not take time off work, so it was Haydn in the morning, Haydn in the evening, Haydn on Saturday—but never, of course, on Sunday.

The fateful afternoon arrived. I went in early and was dismayed to find the Albert Hall almost full. Why were so many people there? I could see the amazing Sisters from the All Hallows' Convent and their brilliant students in the middle of the hall. Had I gone mad? What had happened to my dread of audiences when I agreed to this ordeal?

Sweaty palms, racing pulse—I could cope with that. But my hands were shaking. I couldn't go through with it. But how to escape? A sudden illness? That was the coward's way out. I had to do it.

The concert began. Each of the grade prize winners gave an excellent performance. But an even higher standard would be expected from diploma winners. Walking up the steps to the stage, I took a sideways glance at the audience. *These people,* I thought, *are not here to enjoy a performance of Haydn. They're listening for every weakness—uneven runs, phrasing problems, timing problems, unobserved dynamics, poorly executed ritards—what else could they think up?* I wanted the stage to collapse and bury me.

I adjusted the piano seat and placed my music on the rack. The first chord sounded all right. The second chord—no problems. Could I make it? It was legato, so I didn't have to raise my hands. "Thank you, Haydn," I said, "for writing it that way." But the last page—I had forgotten about the staccato passage! I lifted my hands, but they came down on to the wrong notes. Catastrophe! More wrong notes. How could shaking hands get it right? Would I be able to finish the piece? Fortunately, the last few lines were legato and I raced through them to the end. The audience applauded politely, but I wondered what they were thinking. 'How did such a dill get the prize?' '*My* student could have done far better.' 'I'll bet she did a teacher's diploma. They don't have to be good performers.'

I had done my best, but I sensed my audience was against me. If only I could have explained what had happened, that it was not my fault! But they would probably have told me not to make excuses. That was the kind of thing Father would say. Well, they could think what they liked.

Coming down from the platform, I saw the Licentiate winner approaching—a tall, fair-haired girl, slightly older than I was, who walked with an enviable composure. We acknowledged each other without speaking.

I heaved a deep sigh as I went back to my seat, wondering how the girl on stage would interpret the Bach I should have played. The first note sounded. I had never heard the piece before. Where was that program? I could not believe it! After all this, the girl was not playing my piece, but Bach's Prelude and Fugue in C Minor, Book 1. All that pain because of someone else's incompetence. If only I could have put my hands around the throat of that office secretary! No, I'd have done it verbally. "Do you realize the humiliation you've caused me?" But the secretary would probably have been a nice person and become upset. Then I'd have felt guilty and apologized.

It was a dilemma I could not resolve. I wanted justice for myself, but I wanted people to like me. Life was so unfair. I was constantly being blamed for things that were not my fault. Even my fighting spirit, which Father condemned, I had inherited from him. I was supposed to be gentle, like Deborah and Mother, and just accept whatever was dished up to me. But to do that would be like giving up on life itself. I could not do it.

CHAPTER 19

A Frightening Intruder

Ann Street Presbyterian Church sat on a grassy hill, which sloped steeply down to a busy city road. A broad concrete ramp was at the side. Twenty yards back from the church's front wall, which contained the main entrance door, a section of the building extended out towards the ramp, thereby forming an L shape. It had large Gothic style doors. This entrance was near the front pews. Further in, an elevated area contained the pulpit in the center and the choir stalls on either side. The organ was against the back wall. For three years I practiced in the evening on this instrument.

Brisbane was having a heatwave and I had been in an air-conditioned office all day. Even to go home—to a house which caught whatever breeze there was, did not fill me with delight. But I could hardly bear the thought of going into a building that had been closed all day. "You have to stick at things," Mother would say. In our family, only physical incapacity was accepted as an excuse for non-performance of a duty—even when it was a self-imposed obligation.

I dragged my feet up the ramp and put my key into the lock. "Ouch!" I said, pulling my hand away. The metal had fired in the afternoon sun. I thought of poor Grandfather, spending all his working life stoking train engines. I wrapped a handkerchief around my fingers and pulled the door open. Hot, stale air escaped. Should I close the door? To do so would be like locking myself in an oven. But it would be dark before I had finished practicing. The only building nearby housed the church offices, which would soon be empty. The risk was too great. From inside, I pulled the heavy door closed.

Above the organ was a large mirror, reflecting the small amount of light allowed in by the narrow windows. Raising a limp arm I switched on the fan at the side of the mirror, then used most of my remaining strength to lift the solid wooden cover. The power generated by the organ and its lights raised the temperature still further. My forehead felt wet, and looking up at my reflection, I smiled pitifully at my hair hanging in strings.

Although the organ was small compared to that at Albert Street Methodist, its tone was of high quality, and I was grateful to have the use of such a fine instrument. However, the little fan was not equal to its task that night. Its tiny turbulence barely stirred the heavy air as my gratitude evaporated. I picked up a church news sheet that lay crumpled on the floor and waved it weakly.

"This is hopeless," I said aloud. "There must be a decent fan somewhere. I'm going to raid this building."

I splashed myself with tepid water from the tap marked 'cold' in a nearby kitchen. Then my dripping hands felt around in dark corners and unlocked cupboards. Tea-towels, crockery, saucepans, brass polish, brooms, rags—but nothing that felt like a fan. Perhaps I wasn't meant to practice that night. Yet to give up when the going was tough was not in my nature. I felt worthwhile only when I had achieved the impossible. The heat was just another challenge.

Back at the organ, I opened a Mendelssohn sonata, stumbled through the first movement, and fell forward onto the lower keyboard. With the stops still on, it was a horrible sound. When my ears could stand it no longer, I raised my body and shouted into the empty church "I won't let this beat me!" as I stood up and strode to the door. Putting my fingers around the handle, I stopped. "Please

God," I prayed, "protect me." I opened the door, and it was dark.

A faint breeze came in, and I walked down the ramp to the footpath to cool myself. People were passing in the street, taking no notice of me. Why would a person wander in to a church anyway, other than to pray or to admire the architecture? Leaving the door open this time, I returned to the organ and set the stops for the second movement of my sonata. I let out a cry. A large insect had landed on my left hand. "Get away!" I screamed as I grabbed the news sheet and brushed it off.

The church was silent. I sat motionless for several minutes and then took in a deep breath. Above the sound of the sigh I heard a creak. Most of the church was in darkness, but I could see a shape a few rows from the front as I looked around. It did not move. Picking up my handbag, I ran towards the door. Still, the shape did not move. Was it someone asleep? I crept forward, but now I could see right through the shape. I was staring at a shadow!

That was my last fright for the evening, I decided. Nothing more would disturb me. But just to make sure, I coaxed my hot, tired legs up into the pulpit. It gave a commanding view of the dimly-lit building. What would it be like, I wondered, to address a large congregation? I opened the massive Bible and read aloud the opening verses of the Epistle to the Hebrews. Thrilling to the majesty of the words, I paused for effect at appropriate points and looked up from the page to imaginary people in the pews. As my voice echoed in the empty building, I began to understand why Father loved to preach. It was a feeling of power perhaps even greater than I experienced when filling Albert Street Methodist with the sound of my playing. I almost forgot my earlier fears, but I took one final look around the church, noting where the shadows were and listening for strange sounds. There were none.

In a relaxed state, I could play my pieces properly. Each one was followed by a trip to the kitchen, where I saturated my upper body. Back at the organ, I looked up and laughed again at my reflection. Even if there were an intruder, what man would be interested in such a hideous sight? The emptiness of the building now gave me a feeling of peace. I was a child of God, in his Church, preparing myself to do his work.

My pieces concluded, I flicked through the Presbyterian Hymn book to practice some sight-reading. I stopped suddenly. Floating above the smells of the building came an odor, distasteful and sharp. It startled me. What was it? The horrible smell of beer I remembered when passing the Walka pub. *But how did it get into the church?* My mind was racing. That smell could only come from one source—a human! I listened. Then gasped. Behind my left shoulder—the sounds of heavy breathing! My body froze.

"How are you tonight, love?" The voice sent terror through my body. I could not move or breathe. Frantic thoughts jostled one another in a scramble for acceptance. It was no use screaming—the street was too far away. I didn't think about God, or about praying for rescue. I needed a weapon. The metronome! That would make a dint in the man's skull. From the position of his voice, he didn't sound very tall. Another thought: *should I try to reason with him? Or suggest that we go somewhere more comfortable? If I could get him out of the building, I might have a chance.*

I waited. There was no movement. Nothing except the sound of that breathing and the smell of those horrible fumes. Slowly I turned my head. An unshaven man in bedraggled clothes stared at me. His eyes were bleary, and he held himself upright by leaning on a choir stall. Was a man more or less dangerous when drunk? Coming from a family of teetotalers, I did not know.

"Why did you come in?" I asked. It seemed a silly question, but I couldn't think of anything else.

"I… um… I like… music… Is this a big piano?"

He put an arm out and I thought he was going to grab me. I slid towards the far end of the organ stool and put my hand on the metronome. He looked straight at me. The corners of his mouth turned upwards. He was trying to smile!

At that moment, I realized I would be incapable of striking him. It was not only that I had never hit anyone in my life, or that I hated violence because I had received so much of it. For the first time ever, I saw a vulnerable man. He needed something from me, but unlike Father and Mr. Stewart, he would not attack me to get it. I didn't know what he wanted, but a part of me longed to reach out to him.

He sat down on the organ stool with his back to the keys. He was too close to me. I panicked.

"It's very hot," I said. "I'm going outside to get some air." Pushing past his legs I dashed through the choir stalls, down the steps and out the door, then ran down the ramp to the brightly-lit footpath. Maybe God was looking after me. But where was my visitor? I turned around and saw him staggering towards me.

A middle-aged man in a business suit was passing. Should I call out for help? But that could be more dangerous. There was no one else on the footpath. I decided to run for the corner, but the drunk man had caught up with me. This time he was not smiling.

"It's been nice meeting you," I said, "but I've got an exam soon, so I'd better go in and do some practice."

Without waiting for his response, I ran around him and back up the ramp, slammed the door and fell in a heap into the nearest pew. My heart was pounding, and I was gasping for breath.

Eventually, I stretched out full length on the polished timber and looked up at the unlit lights and the dark ceiling. The church had, throughout history, been seen as a place of refuge, but how shaky that refuge could be! With the door secured, I felt triumphant at having outwitted my visitor. But then I pictured him on the footpath, perhaps leaning against the fence. Maybe he was lonely, and seeing me was the high point of his day. *Had I misjudged him? Should I have spoken kindly to him or even taken him for a cup of coffee around the corner in Albert Street?* I would never know.

The little fan was still churning and the organ lights invited me back, but I'd had enough for one night. After switching everything off and closing the heavy cover, I trudged towards the door I had slammed. Not wanting to see the man again, either through fear or guilt, I decided to take a different exit. But there was no sign of him.

Would he have hurt me? Probably not. But later, as I walked through my front gate, my dampened dress covered with soot from the train, I made a firm resolve, "I'll never leave that door open again!"

CHAPTER 20

"We're Moving to Melbourne"

I had just come home from yet another late practice. It had not been very productive, but I didn't have the sense to stop and return another time when I was fresh. I flopped onto the settee. Father was at a meeting, Deborah was working, and the young ones were in bed. I had Mother to myself.

"I have some important news for you," she said. "We're going to be living in Melbourne."

"What?" I said, jerking my body upright. "Anyway, who's 'we'?"

"Well, your father and I, of course, and Ruth and Jennifer. You and Deborah will have to decide what you want to do."

"Why Melbourne of all places?"

"They offered him a position as Assistant Director of Evangelism."

"I suppose it's a promotion," I said cynically.

"Well, he won't get much more money, but he feels there'll be greater scope for his talents in a large city."

"Does Deborah know?"

"She won't be off duty till tomorrow morning. I'll tell her then."

So typical of Father, I thought, *not bothering to discuss it with Deborah and me. He probably just announced it to Mother too.*

But life without Father—what bliss! No more physical cruelty. No more humiliation in front of other people. No more verbal abuse. No more living in dread of his arrival home at night. I would be free! I began to think about the practical issues. *Where would I live?*

I assumed the house would be let, or even sold if Father was a success down south. *Would Grandma Lewis have me?* Despite her dominating personality, she was not cruel—like her son. I laughed a lot when I was with her. Nothing she said made any sense, but she assumed the world agreed with her.

Yes, I would definitely stay in Brisbane, but not say anything in the meantime. I did not want to influence Deborah's decision, and I wanted to time my announcement to have the maximum effect on Father.

Breakfast the next morning was particularly tense. Deborah had just been told the news and she looked shaken.

"Have you thought of all the disruption to our lives?" I said to Father. "Changes of schools for Ruth and Jennifer—to say nothing of the loss of friendships?"

"Of course, I've thought of everything," he replied. "You girls don't realize how much I think about you. Your Mother and I pray for you every night. But when God calls, his servant must obey—like the Old Testament prophets."

"Well, Deb, what do you think of that?" I asked as soon as we were alone. "As though he hasn't caused us enough problems already! What will you do?" I asked. "Will you stay at the General?"

"I might be able to finish my training at a hospital in Melbourne. The whole thing is such a nuisance."

I gave a lot of thought to how I would announce my decision. I pictured the look on Father's face. He probably believed that since no man would ever want me, he would control me till he died. Well, he would have to think again. The hour of my triumph was approaching.

After dinner that night, when Father seemed in a tolerable mood, I looked straight at him.

"I have something to tell you. I have lived 'under your roof,' as you call it, for twenty-three years. I have been subject to your verbal and physical attacks, more than any other girl I have ever known. I do not accept that I am more evil than everyone else. When you go to Melbourne, I will not come with you. I will live the rest of my life as I choose to, and there's nothing you can do about it."

"You won't last five minutes! Who would want you anyway?"

"I've always been happy staying with Grandma Lewis when you've been away on holiday."

"I can easily put a stop to that," he sneered.

"You sound as though you'll actually miss me!"

"That's nothing to do with it. You need my guidance."

"Well, whether I need it or not, I won't be there to get it."

I went to bed with a feeling of elation I had never experienced before. I had been strong enough to stand up to Father—to tell him exactly what I thought of him! If I could do that, I could do anything.

Mother woke me the following day with my orange juice. She seemed worried. Was it that she thought I couldn't survive on my own? My mother and my sisters were the only security I had ever known. I had always found it extremely difficult to make friends. Also, although Mother and I were not close, she did everything she could to make life easy for me at a practical level—washing, ironing, sewing. I was too embarrassed to tell anyone outside the family how she spoilt me. And despite her inability to love me the way I needed her to, she disciplined herself to be interested in what I was doing and to spend time talking to me. It even seemed on some occasions that when I was upset, she shared the feeling with me. What she really thought of me I could never fathom.

"You don't think I can make it by myself, do you?"

"That's not true! You're an intelligent girl. You could easily manage all the things I do for you." There were tears in her eyes. She wanted me to go with her!

Throughout the day, I began to think, not about life without Father, but life without Mother and the girls. *Was I really strong enough to face the world alone?* It was not the practical tasks that worried me. It was the feeling of having no boundaries, no reference points, no one to tell me I was right or wrong. *What if I made a mistake—messed up a relationship? Who would bail me out? Who would comfort me the way Mother could?*

The question of relationships had troubled me ever since my early teenage years. I had an intense longing to be loved, but none of the boys at our church were remotely interested in me. I thought this was because of my strange personality and assumed I was destined to be single for the rest of my life. But years later, I was talking to a man the same age as me who had grown up in the church our family attended. I mentioned my problem to him, and he could not understand it. He said to me, "As boys, we knew we could never approach you or your sisters. With your father being the way he was, we would say to each other, 'It's hands off the Lewis girls.'"

For days, I fluctuated between a longing to escape from Father's prison and a fear that I would never survive without my family. Then one day, the fear overwhelmed me. Life on my own suddenly seemed terrifying. But I had already announced my decision, and I couldn't go back on it now. That would be the ultimate humiliation.

I said nothing for several days. Father ignored me, looking in a different direction whenever we were in the same room. Mother was quiet. I didn't know what she was thinking.

One afternoon, I looked at her intently, and something deep inside me snapped. I knew I had to have her by my side.

"I will go with you," I said quietly.

"That's nice," she replied, without any display of emotion. I was desperately disappointed that she had not reacted with pleasure. But then I wondered whether she secretly thought I had made the wrong decision. Perhaps if she had been me, she would have jumped at the chance to escape.

"I'm not going to tell Father yet," I said. "Could you do it for me, but leave it till the last possible minute? He'll be insufferable when he finds out he's won."

"I knew you'd come to your senses," said Father a few days later. At least Mother had tried to wait, but perhaps her conscience had got the better of her.

I had managed to get a transfer to Melbourne in the Commonwealth Public Service. But I knew the work in the new office would be as uninspiring as it had been in Brisbane. My next task was to find a competent organ teacher. I had done well in my grade examinations for the organ, and I was planning to do my Associate Diploma the following year. I would want a teacher whom I liked as well as Mr. Day. I certainly did not want another man like Father in my life. I heard about an Italian organist, Mario Rizzo, who taught at a large Anglican church in the city. Several of his students had done well at diploma level, and I decided to give him a try.

Over the next few weeks, while we were busy packing, Mother seemed lost in her own thoughts. I would have given anything to know what they were, but she had a way of barring any intrusion into her private world.

On our departure, we waved goodbye to our cream-painted home. We had known much pain there. But the four of us could remember times of happiness too, times when we had created a magical world in which Father's prohibitions and punishments were temporarily forgotten.

Our means of transport to Melbourne was by train. The overnight journey to Sydney began at South Brisbane Station, where we found the train waiting for us. It was strange to see the rear of the guard's van backed up against a platform. This meant the train could only go in one direction—away from our home. It carried the State of New South Wales insignia but could easily have passed for the local variety. However, the next day in Sydney, we changed to the "Spirit of Progress," which was another world for us. There was so much space, and the soft colors of the walls and seats contrasted the Queensland browns and blacks. We expected the familiar jolt to begin our journey, but did not realize we were moving until we saw the people on the platform disappearing.

We girls explored as much of the train as we were allowed to. Then after a while, we stuck our noses to the windows to catch our first glimpse of sheep. We had never been to a rural area and fell in love with the little white shapes spread out across the grassy hills. They barely seemed to move, except for the few who found themselves a little too close to the flying rattler.

Our journey ended in Melbourne at Spencer Street Station. I was expecting it to be like Central in Brisbane, but the mass of crisscrossing tracks indicated that this was indeed a big city. No wonder Father wanted to make his mark in it. A friend with a station wagon drove us to our new home in North Balwyn. Like all the other houses we could see, it was brick. In Brisbane, only rich people had brick homes.

While the rest of us were unpacking, Father spread out maps and timetables on the only floor area not covered with our belongings.

"We'll have to be in bed early," he said. "We have to take two buses to get to the church tomorrow. We'll leave at eight o'clock."

"Oh, Peter!" said Mother, in a tone of exasperation normally reserved for her children. "Surely we could try one of the local churches—just till your car arrives."

"No," he replied. "This is the place where I need to be. I must make myself known immediately."

After the service the following morning, Father introduced himself to the minister, David Landel, who greeted him warmly. He was in his early thirties, though his demeanor carried the authority of a much older man. I was next to Father, but he made no attempt to introduce me.

"Congratulations on your appointment," said Mr. Landel, shaking Father's hand. "We're so pleased you've decided to join us. This must be your daughter," he said, looking at me and smiling.

As well as a pleasant manner, Mr. Landel had a voice like a radio announcer. It was such a contrast to the sound of Father's harsh, scratchy tone. Surely, he would now have the sense to try to moderate it.

"Until I'm better known in the churches," said Father, obviously unaware of what he sounded like, "I'd appreciate being able to preach here whenever you could arrange it."

Mr. Landel looked stunned. "We have quite a few preachers in the circuit. I couldn't guarantee you anything on a regular basis."

"Well, whatever you can manage, I'd be grateful. I've been told that this is an evangelical church. I trust my information is correct."

"We… we do preach the gospel," replied the minister, a little taken aback.

"Do you make appeals?" asked Father, with a tone of urgency.

"You mean to invite people to come forward down the aisles—Billy Graham style?"

"Yes, of course," said Father. "What other way is there?"

Mr. Landel sighed. "Perhaps Melbourne people are a little more reserved than you are up north," he said with a smile.

Father would not be put off. "So you don't give any invitations at all?"

"I didn't say that," the minister replied in an even tone. "I tell the congregation that they can see me in the vestry at any time after the service."

"And how many do?" snapped Father.

"From time to time, quite a few."

"The New Testament demands a public confession of faith," Father said in a peremptory tone.

"The Confirmation Service *is* such a confession." Mr. Landel sounded like he was about to put Father in his place. I was looking forward to that.

"That's just a formality," said Father. "At least it is in most churches."

Mr. Landel looked across at an elderly woman using her stick to get down the steps and rushed to help her.

I was relieved. Although I had hoped Mr. Landel would get the better of Father, I realized I did not want the kindly minister to think less of our family. Mother was already making herself known to a group of women in the foyer, who seemed just as friendly as the church women in Brisbane. In any case, Mother had such a gracious manner she was accepted in any company.

Later, I told Father I would have organ lessons at an Anglican church with a Mr. Rizzo, who had come from one of the Italian cathedrals.

"I don't know much about that lot," he said, "but I'm not happy about it. You know they're like Catholics."

"I don't think I'll be theologically contaminated just having music lessons there," I said tartly.

He glared at me but did not reply.

It seemed that whatever I did, no matter how well-thought-out or well-intentioned, the dark cloud of my father's presence distorted my reality. I had tried to escape from it, but it overwhelmed me, turning my natural energy and vitality into fear—that the world would never want me. I did not belong.

CHAPTER 21

Lovestruck in the Organ Loft

After arranging a time with Mr. Rizzo for my first lesson, I visited his church, which held a weekly lunch-hour service. I fought my way through the crowds surging in the opposite direction. The church was huge and like so many buildings in Melbourne, had the old-world charm of Victorian architecture. As I entered, I tried to walk in a dignified manner befitting a worshipper in an Anglican church. On one side of the building, the sun and the black-outlined figures in the stained-glass windows met in a joyful embrace, the strains of the organ solemnizing their union. The magnificent vaulted arches, the massive pillars, and the ornate white altar created a sense of majesty. But I could not help feeling that the God worshipped in such a place was remote from ordinary people. At least the building did not suggest a God of judgment, which I always felt at our church at Walka, but I still craved the loving God of Albert Street Methodist.

Mr. Rizzo played for the service, and the sound of the mighty organ seemed to resonate from every crevice in the building. It came from the chancel, from the nave, curled around pillars, floated upwards to the cherubs high above the altar, and floated downwards to the congregation. I tried to sing the hymns, but my vocal cords refused. All I could do was listen to that thrilling sound. I had been planning to introduce myself in person to my new teacher after the service. But I felt that in my state of ecstasy, I would not even be coherent.

Throughout the afternoon, I found difficulty concentrating on my work. I had obtained a transfer in the Commonwealth Public Service, but being in any government department was for me a source of boredom and irritation. I wondered whether it would be more satisfying in private enterprise. However, because of my political views, I was not thrilled by the idea of working to increase shareholders' bank accounts. In a year, when I had my diploma, I was determined to go somewhere to complete my secondary education at night and train to be a teacher. Of course, I would have to keep this a secret from Mother and Father.

As I lay in bed that night, the sounds of the organ floated in and out of my consciousness. I had heard of reverberation but had never before experienced it. I could hardly wait till I was at the console of that magnificent instrument. I just wanted to play a chord, raise my hands, and wait for the sound to come back to me. Then I could imagine that I was in the great tradition of Cathedral organists.

Would Mr. Rizzo like me? I knew of his ability, both as a teacher and a performer. He often gave recitals at his church and also at the Town Hall. But what was he really like as a person? He had agreed to take me, presumably based on my examination results. But I hoped he would not expect me to be brilliant or do what Miss Grant did—give me music that was beyond my capabilities. Should I tell him that I was not talented—just a hard worker? Or would he be skillful enough to work this out for himself? Fearing that my unacceptable personality would sooner or later destroy all my relationships, creating a good impression at a first meeting was important to me.

A thunderstorm broke just as I arrived for my lesson at seven o'clock the following Thursday evening. Flashes of lightning lit the church's wall, changing its color to a silvery grey. I dashed up from the street and across the courtyard. The wind had blown my umbrella inside out, but I held it above my head—to catch water rather than divert it. The cobbles crunched under my sodden shoes, and my soaked cotton dress clung to my body.

I took a flying leap onto the low veranda that jutted out at right angles to the building. There was no light, apart from that provided intermittently from the sky. My handbag and music case fell to the floor as I tried to straighten my umbrella.

The smell of a spicy after-shave lotion startled me. I couldn't see anybody that could own it, and there was no sound to indicate its location.

"Is someone there?" I asked. A low-pitched cough came from the end of the veranda.

"I didn't want to frighten you," said a deep voice. I could just see the outline of a tall, well-built figure walking towards me.

"Here, let me take your umbrella." Mr. Rizzo put his hand on my wrist and held it for a few seconds before sliding his fingers down mine and slowly drawing the umbrella towards him. His skin felt hot. "It will be safe in this corner." *Perhaps more so than his student,* I thought. *What had I let myself in for?*

"I'm sorry the light has gone out," he said with questionable sincerity. "We have to climb twenty-four steps. You go first. In case you fall, I can catch you."

I took a firm grasp of the rough wooden handrail of a spiral staircase surrounded by stone walls. The overhead lights seemed to be minimum wattage. I took a firm grasp of the rough wooden handrail. It was worth the risk of splinters to avoid collapsing into those waiting arms. Round and round we went. I lost all sense of direction. Although we were ascending, we could just as well have been descending to a bottomless void—or going backwards in time.

Mr. Rizzo's footsteps sounded a safe distance below mine, but then the after-shave aroma became uncomfortably intense.

"Be careful at the top," he whispered. "There's a loose floorboard. I'd hate anything to happen to you." I kept a steady pace.

"I'm so sorry there's nowhere we can dry your dress out."

Thank goodness for that, I thought, as I stepped over the floorboard, groping my way along the narrow passage. I looked up at the enormous pipes all around me. At their highest point, they lost themselves in the darkness of the roof. There was a mystery about an organ. It drew into itself the air of the planet, then converted it into a sound that seemed to have its origins in the heavens. Even the upward reach of the pipes suggested a desire to return to that source.

From the loft balcony, the lights shed a soft glow into the vast cavern below. It was a long way down. I could only just see the floor of the building. After changing into my polished organ shoes, I slid along the stool and placed my music on the rack, wondering what the mysterious man would do next.

To the left of the rack was a photograph of the Rizzo family. His wife and three daughters were stunningly beautiful. They had flawless olive complexions, shiny black hair, and teeth as white as ocean foam.

"They're so lovely!" I said, unable to take my eyes from the photo.

I had always hated my fair skin, particularly when it protested visibly at its exposure to a hostile sun. But apart from my feelings of envy at Mediterranean beauty, I felt reassured about my new teacher.

"Yes, I'm a lucky man," he said, looking admiringly at his family. I was ashamed of myself for having misjudged him.

His gaze moved from the photo to my music. "A Bach trio sonata!" he exclaimed. "How delightful. I'll set the stops for you." He stood behind me and leant his body against mine as he reached over to the right and left panels.

This is crazy, I thought. *How can he do this a few feet away from that reminder of family bliss?*

I had recently played the Bach for my seventh-grade examination, and despite being on a strange organ, I managed to get through it without accident. But already, I was trying to work out what I should do. There was no way I would encourage Mr. Rizzo's behavior, even though I had no idea what he was up to. On the other hand, I did not want to register any disapproval, through fear of alienating him. I had come all the way from Brisbane to be his student. I could not afford to wreck things.

"You play the organ very well," he said at the end of the piece. "I'm sure there are other things you do well."

"Well, I think I'm a reasonable pianist," I replied anxiously.

"So you'd like me to teach you?" Mr. Rizzo asked, sliding closer to me on the stool.

"Oh yes," I said, "if you think I'm technically competent."

"There are so many things I could teach you."

"Well, you have an excellent reputation."

Surely, I thought, *he must get the message soon.*

I played a few more pieces, and the warm hands rested on mine at the end of each.

"I think you need to expand your horizons," he said in a whisper. I was not sure whether he was referring to my playing or my personal life.

Feelings of relief and thankfulness flooded over me as he produced a piece of his own. It was by a modern French composer. My teacher obviously liked contemporary music. I loathed it, but there was no way I would tell him that. He moved his body quickly along the seat so that his leg bumped against mine.

"I'm so sorry," I said as I slid even more quickly away from him.

"I didn't realize you wanted to play the piece."

"Don't worry about that," he said, smiling at my discomfort. "I think we're going to enjoy our time together."

He looked deep into my eyes in a way that made me feel uncomfortable. It was an invasive look, as though he believed he had some right of access to my soul.

"Would you like to hear the walls of the church shake?"

"Oh yes, please!" I had only ever seen brilliant organists at a distance and could hardly wait to see the action close-up.

"I'm playing this at the Town Hall next week." The music pages, plastered with semiquavers, looked more black than white.

From the first note, I could not believe what I was seeing. The virtuoso's fingers were moving so quickly I felt I had blurred vision. Then I looked down at the pedal board, where feet were flying from one end to the other. I could not understand how the human body could move at such a speed. I was mesmerized by the technical brilliance, but beyond that, I felt I understood something of my teacher's personality through his playing. He was strong, and he was masterful. Nothing could ever defeat him.

At the conclusion, it took a while to regain my composure.

"I'm lost for words," I said. "That was breathtaking."

"You're so kind to appreciate my humble effort."

I resisted the temptation to challenge the mocking self-deprecation. He gave me another one of those looks. I blushed and turned my head away.

That night I hardly slept. I was confused and almost frightened. My teacher's unusual behavior had begun in the darkness before he had even caught sight of me. So it was clear that he did not have any special attraction to me. That gave me some relief, as did his evident devotion to his family. Compared to them, I was positively plain.

I concluded that he was just a harmless flirt and I would adopt a pleasant but neutral attitude towards him.

Having sorted all that out, I felt I could now concentrate on the hard work ahead of me. However, my teacher's behavior had created a problem, but not in the sense of fear for my safety. All I could think about for the rest of the night was the feel of those caressing hands. No man had ever touched my skin before, except in rage. I could feel myself being drawn into a whirlpool of intense physical desire. It was not only the feel of his flesh that I wanted to experience again. Nor was it just the sight of those piercing black eyes or that mischievous smile. There was something about him that was larger than life. He was brilliant and made all other men I had ever met seem insignificant. He was totally uninhibited—so free in expressing his desires and yet so lacking in any sense of pretense or harsh attitude of dominance that made my life at home such a misery. I wanted to lose myself in him—to become part of that loveliness, that power, that spontaneous zest for life. I wanted him, but I knew I could never have him. Even if he had offered himself to me, there was no way my upbringing would ever have allowed me to respond to him. All I could do was dream... and practice... and dream...

CHAPTER 22

What to Make of This Strange Man?

Our family's church had a small two-manual organ, and I would practice there each night till I dropped from exhaustion. More than anything in my life, I wanted Mr. Rizzo's approval. I wanted him to like me, and to do that, he would have to like my playing. I hated the piece he had given me to learn. How could a person of taste and discernment enjoy music where the notes seemed to be thrown together at random? But I tried to convince myself that since I loved my teacher so much, I could learn to love his music.

I was counting the days till my next lesson. The piece sounded reasonable, but all I could think about was that dark, beautiful face and that caressing voice that made my body tingle. *Would he touch me again?* On Thursday, I stayed in the city after work and tried to eat dinner, but my digestive system was like a volcano. I sipped a cool drink, and it gurgled all the way down into the eruption.

Mr. Rizzo was waiting for me on the church veranda. This time, the light was working, and I looked into his face. Something was wrong; there was no sparkle in his eyes. All the tenderness had gone.

"Good evening," he said, in a voice as cold as the South Pole.

My whole world fell apart. I knew I must have done something wrong. My life was a succession of misdeeds. But what was it this time? It could not have been my playing. He liked that. It must have been something I said or did. I had spoken courteously and called him by his name, as I had been brought up to do. It must have been my behavior. Perhaps he thought I was a prude because I did not respond to him the previous week. But what should I do now?

I went ahead of him up the spiral staircase. This time, he was well behind me as we walked in silence. At the organ, I opened the piece he had given me and waited. He sat as far away from me as he could, still with the surly expression.

"Well, aren't you going to set the stops?" he barked.

"I've been practicing it on flutes," I replied quietly. "I didn't want to try anything heavier while I was still learning it, but do you want something more?"

"Please yourself," he said in a tone of indifference.

I was close to tears, but my hands were steady, and I made a fair attempt at the piece. At the end, I rested my arms on my lap and did not move.

"That was not bad for one week's work."

The tone in his voice was still flat, but at least my playing had not offended him. He then discussed technical details in a manner that sounded like a recorded message. At the end of the lesson, he stood up suddenly.

"Goodnight," he said, his tone unchanged.

I'd had enough. I felt humiliated, and I was furious. I was not going to subject myself to that treatment again.

"Mr. Rizzo," I said in the iciest voice my throat could produce, "do you still want to teach me?"

"Of course," he said, as though he didn't care one way or the other. "I'll see you next week."

That's what you think, I said to myself.

My mind and body were sick. All my hopes—fantasies though I knew them to be—had evaporated in a matter of seconds. I could perhaps have coped with it if only I had known what it was that I had done. At least at home, I knew what my punishments were for in advance. Surely, I had not come all the way to Melbourne to find a man just like Father? Life could not be so cruel.

The next day, I rang all the churches in the city to find out whether their organists took students. There were just a few possible teachers. One of them was a woman. Would I ring her? *Surely, she could not be as horrible as Mr. Rizzo?* I visited her church the following Sunday to see what she was like. Her playing was outstanding. After the service, I sneaked up close to the organ as she was walking down the steps into the body of the church. Her thin lips were tightly drawn, and her partially-dyed blond hair was pulled back in a bun. The expression on her face was so hard I could not imagine ever feeling at ease in her presence.

"Dear God," I prayed that night, "show me what you want me to do about an organ teacher."

I started thinking about Mr. Rizzo again. Perhaps he'd just been through some great tragedy. But then he could have cancelled the lesson, or at least given me some explanation for his unusual behavior. *Was my first lesson just a dream? Did I read more into it than was actually the case?* As I tossed these ideas around, I pictured my teacher on that first night. I was expecting to be furious at the way he had conned me into believing he was such a charming man. Instead, to my astonishment, all the feelings I had developed for him before I had fallen asleep that night came rushing over me. I was in love again! Then I went into a silent rage—but not with him. *How could I have been so stupid? How could I ever trust such a reprehensible creature again?* I was losing my sanity.

There was only one way to solve the problem. I would simply practice hard and turn up at the next lesson. Should he repeat the previous week's behavior, I was out of there for good. I would find a teacher somewhere, even if it meant going back to Brisbane.

I arrived at the usual time. The staircase was lit, and I could hear the organ playing. I wandered into the church and looked up into the loft, where a female student was in the middle of a lesson. *This will be interesting,* I thought. *I'll sit in a pew and watch what happens.* Mr. Rizzo sat at the far end of the organ stool. That was not a good sign. I assumed he treated all his female students the same way, which meant that his impossible mood of the previous week had continued.

At the end of the lesson, he walked ahead of the student down the stairs. I rushed out to the car park and pretended I was just walking in as the two reached the veranda.

The girl left. I still could not tell whether this would be the last lesson I would ever have in that church. I prepared for the worst by saying to myself over and over, *the last one… the last one… you can stick it just one more time… one more time…*

With my heart thumping, I quickly glanced across at Mr. Rizzo. That beautiful smile was there again! Last week was just a bad dream. This time, he put his arms around me and held me tight. I was in heaven. I stood there, like a good girl, without moving. I must have looked like Mother when she would not respond to my affection. If only I could have trusted myself—or my teacher for that matter—I would have given anything to crush him with my tiny arms. Instead, all I allowed myself to do eventually was rest my head against his shoulder.

That must have been enough to convince him that I was happy with him—but if only he had known how happy! As I was a reasonably well-presented young woman, he probably assumed I had one or two male admirers. He could never have imagined that he was the first man I had ever really loved.

The lesson followed much the same pattern as the first, except he seemed even more relaxed and freer to let his hands roam. He must have been pleased that I was a conscientious student in that his pleasure in my company would never be spoilt by having to listen to wrong notes. On the other hand, could I dare to believe that he actually liked me more than his other female students? He certainly seemed distant with the other girl. My hopes soared, but then a horrible thought crossed my mind. What if he were emotionally unstable—and changed from one hour to the next? I hoped and prayed that I was wrong.

CHAPTER 23

"You're a Lovely Girl and a Damn Good Organist"

The following two lessons were pure bliss. My teacher did not actually increase the extent of his affectionate gestures—it was more like a theme with variations. Being a creative genius, he could always surprise me. I was relieved that he had placed a limit on his amorous activities. Otherwise, I would have had to resist him. That might have angered him, and I could not risk that. I don't think he had any idea of his effect on me. To him, the whole thing was just a game. I still could not keep down any food on Thursday nights, but that was a small price to pay for being with the man I loved. I had almost forgotten the disastrous evening three weeks earlier and assumed that Mr. Rizzo had been deeply hurt by something or someone that day.

A funny incident occurred in our local church the following Sunday, and I was wondering how to describe it to him at my next lesson. I was already smiling as I walked onto the church veranda, but my smile vanished instantly. *Oh no!* I thought. *He's having another "off" night.* At least I knew what to expect this time, but that did not lessen my suffering. To see that magic face transformed into something I could hardly bear to look at filled me with overwhelming pain. All my anticipation of the lovely things he might do to me that night—what a hollow memory they were now.

I had decided never to display any negative feelings to him again, so I pretended everything was all right. But as the lesson went on,

I knew I had to do something—anything that would rescue me from being sucked into this black hole. I had an inspiration. I would change his mood!

"Last Sunday at our church," I said in a breezy voice, "the choir was singing an anthem. It was building up to a climax when the sopranos in the front row stopped singing and started giggling. The harmony parts behind them didn't realize what was going on, so they continued. The conductor couldn't see what was happening either. We heard a dog bark, and the minister's cat came tearing into the building through a side door. He put on the brakes by digging his claws into the carpet right in the middle of the church. The poor minister blushed and waved frantically to a steward to remove the animal. By this time, the choir and the whole congregation had dissolved in laughter."

I had hardly looked at Mr. Rizzo—I did not want to risk being put off my story.

When I finished, there was a deathly silence. I stared straight ahead.

"You can work on the Vaughan-Williams, and I'll see you next week." With that, he was gone.

At that moment, I hated him. *Right,* I said to myself, *that's it. This man is unworthy of my love.* I could not excuse him the second time on the grounds of having had a bad day—nothing could justify this kind of behavior. I packed up my things and walked slowly down the stairs with a heavy sigh and an even heavier heart. *Would I stay with him? How often would he be like this?*

I tossed for hours in bed that night, trying to find some possible explanation for what he had done. This time, I knew it was not my fault. One thing I resolved—if I decided to stay with him, I would never again try to humor him. In that state of mind, he was unreachable. I had heard of the artistic temperament and the terrible depression such people could suffer, but I never imagined they would be cruel. I pictured them curled up in a corner, not inflicting their misery on other people. In our family, getting in moods was forbidden. "You are not allowed to cast a gloom over the household," Mother would say.

My anger subsided a little, and I could feel myself gradually coming under his spell again—distant though it was. If he did suffer from depression, I wanted to help him somehow, to be able to comfort him. But I didn't know how. I tried to imagine what the world would be like if there were no great artists. It was unthinkable. Mr. Rizzo was indeed a genius; he could play the most technically complex music at sight—pieces that would take most people a year to learn. And his mastery of both the keyboard and the pedal board was awesome.

Until then, I had imagined I loved this man for his power, spontaneity, and beautiful face. But I began thinking about something I had overheard Mother say, "Women tend to fall in love with men who are like their fathers." In some ways, Mr. Rizzo was even worse than my own father, whose temper was at least predictable. But from another perspective, a different picture emerged. With my teacher, each episode in his life seemed completely isolated from all others. Whenever he saw me the week after we'd had a bad night, I could tell he had no memory of the previous week. By contrast, Father prided himself on remembering every transgression I had ever committed, going back to when I was four. The greatest difference between them was that the only thing Father admired about me was my abilities. When he was functioning normally, my teacher seemed to like the whole package.

I swung between two states. On the one hand, whenever I remembered his hurtful looks, his frosty voice, and his overall hostility towards me, I promised myself I would never think about him again. On the other hand, I fantasized that by loving him, I could solve the problem and enjoy those feelings of love forever. Eventually, love won out.

Each day and night, my thoughts were consumed by feelings of overwhelming intensity. It was not as though there could ever be any hope of fulfilling my desires, but having been starved of love for my whole life, just to have feelings like this for the first time ever was pure bliss.

The following week, Mr. Rizzo was back to his usual adorable self. One of my diploma pieces was a Handel concerto. I had just finished playing it when he walked around behind the organ stool and put both arms around me. I sat motionless, wishing the moment would never end.

"That was beautiful—just like you," he said. I could have given him almost anything.

I broke my own rule and put my hands on his.

"I want you to enter the ABC's Vocal and Concerto Competition," he announced in a manner which assumed my consent.

"No!" I screamed in panic. "I'm so sorry," I said, lowering the volume. "It's just that I can't play in public, even when the audience comprises friendly church people. As for playing with an orchestra— it's out of the question."

"You always underestimate yourself, my dear," he said, stroking my hair. "You have a lot of ability that you still haven't used."

"You are completely wrong," I said. "I get there by sheer hard work."

"How much practice do you do a night?" he asked.

He sat down almost on top of me but facing away from the organ.

"Three hours," I said.

He swung around and stared at me, open-mouthed. "I can't believe that! Most of my students are lucky if they do an hour."

This was my chance to convince him.

"I have to," I said in a tone of resignation. "I simply do not have musical talent."

At that point, my teacher seemed to accept that I would not be entering the Concerto Competition. But in case he ever raised the matter again, I took the opportunity to let him know that I was planning to leave Melbourne for good.

"You are a delight!" he said, taking my hand and putting it to his lips. "I don't suppose I can claim to be proud of you, but I'm proud to know you. You're a lovely girl and a damn good organist."

He looked into my eyes, and there was almost a suggestion of sadness. I had no idea what that was about.

CHAPTER 24

The Last Straw

A lovely girl and a damn good organist. I said the words over and over again. I wanted to write them on a plaque and hang them on my bedroom wall. *A lovely girl—did he really mean it?* If he was right, how could my parents, who thought they knew me better than anyone else, have been so wrong? They had blamed me for things that were not my fault. I had inherited the wrong personality. I was a fighter; they said I should be submissive. I got steamed up in an argument; they said I should be gentle. On top of that, I didn't smile enough, my speaking voice was too loud, I used my hands too much; in short, I did not fit the biblical description of a woman.

I blamed God. Why did he make me 'masculine' if he had created me female? But Mr. Rizzo had told me that I was "all woman." Supposing he was right about me. Should I get away from home? Go overseas? Try to find a special man who could love me? Up to that point, the only men who had been interested in me were those nobody else wanted. Having fallen under the spell of an amazingly gifted man, I would find it challenging to be with somebody ordinary. But if my parents turned out to be correct, I would have to change radically.

I practiced smiling sweetly in front of the mirror, but I looked like someone recovering from an illness. Then I had an imaginary conversation, with my arms held tightly at my side. This time I looked like a puppet with its arms disconnected from the strings.

I tried speaking softly, but it didn't sound like me, and in any case, I could only use a quiet voice when I didn't feel passionate about something—and that was hardly ever. If I couldn't be loved for the person I was, I might as well give up.

I arranged to get a lift home with Father after work that afternoon. He said he would drive around the block and pick me up in front of my building. "Make sure you're waiting for me!" he snapped.

At four o'clock, I had a phone call from Mr. Rizzo. "Congratulations," he said. "You've passed! You are now an A.Mus.A."

"I … can't believe it!" I gasped. "The exam was such a disaster."

Although my playing had been accurate, the attitude of the two examiners was less than friendly. I remembered the charming examiner from London whom I had for my piano diploma and was expecting something similar. To my horror, one of the examiners was the surly woman I had seen at one of the city churches when I was looking for a new teacher. Her manner of addressing me was in keeping with her appearance. The male examiner, with a pinched nose and an almost invisible mouth, spent most of the time down in the body of the church so he could hear the sound while the woman glared at me in the loft.

"I never had any doubt that you would make it," said Mr. Rizzo in his most seductive voice. "Would you like to come and get the report?" *Did he really have to ask?*

At 5.06 pm, with my hands shaking, I put my time card in the Bundy clock and dashed out the door. I did not bother to think about Mother's criticism of how I walked. The peak-hour crowds became a side-vision blur as I flew along the street. If I had knocked one or two bodies over, it would not have mattered.

At the church, I raced across the courtyard and through the door. A mischievous smile greeted me, and strong arms were wrapped around me so tightly I could hardly breathe. My teacher and I sat down, and he held my hand as we went through the report. I had received only minimum pass marks, and we both thought the comments were ridiculous. But it didn't matter. I was happy.

"I know you don't want to do any further study on the organ," he said. "But I'd love to see you some time in the loft when I'm playing for a service." Those black eyes were looking deep into my soul, and once more, I was a captive.

I suddenly realized how late it was and looked at my watch. "I have to go now," I said abruptly, without explanation. To my horror, I had just become aware that I had missed Father's deadline for picking me up. I knew he would go completely berserk when I was not there to meet him. I could not ring him because he would have already left his office. I pictured him driving round and round the block, getting more furious by the second. I raced to the train and just managed to fall into a carriage. Then I ran all the way from the station.

When I arrived home, Father was waiting for me, with that horrible scowl I knew so well. "Get in there!" he said, pointing to his bedroom. I wondered why he did not go to the lounge if he wanted to give me a lecture. I thought perhaps he did not want to humiliate me in front of the family. I walked in and sat on the bed, ready to apologize and explain what had happened.

"What do you think you're doing?" he roared. "Get up!"

"I was just about to tell you what happened," I said defiantly.

"I'm not interested in your excuses." He opened the cupboard door and was groping around at the bottom. I couldn't work out what he was looking for. What did he pull out but the cane! That horrible thing he had beaten me with from when I was a young child, right through my teenage years—he had brought it all the way from Brisbane!

Until that moment, I had never tried to reason with Father when he was in a rage. He always interpreted any attempt at self-justification as a challenge to his authority. But this time I was determined to stand my ground.

"The only reason I was not waiting for you was that I had received the most amazing news. I passed my—"

"I told you I'm not interested," he shouted. "Bend over the bed!"

I was speechless with rage, but I obeyed.

"You're being a smart Alec now," he said. "Lift your skirt." Again, I obeyed. "And your petticoat." All I had left on were my panties, suspender belt, and stockings. I felt as helpless and vulnerable as I had the first time he'd beaten me on the buttocks when I'd tripped and broke some eggs when I was just seven. To Father, I was still that evil child, forever in rebellion against him and against God.

"You defied me!" he said. "This will teach you." He raised the cane and brought it down with all his might. "Round and round the block I drove. Round and round!"

His voice was getting louder, the repeated word coinciding with the stinging sensation of the cane. What kind of a monster was this man? I hated him as I had never hated anything or anyone in my life before.

Something inside me snapped as I walked in pain across the hallway to my bedroom. Until then, I had believed, deep down, that if I could have been a different person, my life at home would have been happy. Now I wondered whether my father had used me simply to release his uncontrollable anger. I did not know what he was angry with, but there could be no connection between my inadequacies and his unleashed fury. To be beaten at twenty-three was beyond all reason, even if I had committed a crime. I was ashamed to have inherited even one single gene from such a man.

Although I was never sexually abused, it was suggested to me years later that there were sexual overtones in my father's behavior. Whether this was the case, I will never know.

Shortly afterwards, the man who had caused me such pain left to attend a meeting at the Department of Evangelism. I determined to settle this issue once and for all.

"Mother," I said in a tone of urgency as I strode into the kitchen, "I need to talk to you."

In a noncommittal manner, she sat down next to me. "You heard what happened between Father and me. You always told me that he would beat me till I was twenty-one. I'm two years past that age, and he has done it again."

Mother was a person of principle. I had never known her to lie to me. Despite her remote manner, I believed that she did care for me at some level. Surely, this was the occasion for her to take a stand—to defend me against the man she should never have married.

She did not look at me. "The age of twenty-one," she said in a detached voice, "is something that is recognized by the State, but it has no relevance in this home. As long as you're under his roof, your father has the right to discipline you in any way he chooses."

I could not believe what I was hearing. It was the ultimate betrayal. Father, in my eyes, was a nonperson. But Mother! How could she do such a thing to her own flesh and blood? I stood up abruptly and stared at her. She winced at the sight of the fury in my face, which had never before been directed at her. But I did not move; I did not change my expression. I would stay there until one of us cracked. Slowly she got up and, without looking at me, left the room.

I had lost everything. My only source of love, limited though it was, had gone. Of course, my sisters loved me, but I had been dumped on them—they did not select me.

Why did I find love so hard to get? Most girls my age had boyfriends or at least parents who loved them. I thought of Mr. Rizzo again. He was strange and unpredictable, but at least he had some kind of feeling for me. I began to cry. The whole thing was so absurd. My only source of comfort was an organ teacher playing for a church service! But if that was all I had, I could not turn my back on it.

I arrived at the church early and went up to the organ loft.

"Are you all right?" Mr. Rizzo whispered, looking into my red eyes. I just nodded. I did not tell him what had happened—in fact, no one outside our family knew what went on behind the walls of our home. But just to be with him again was enough for me to believe that there was hope for me.

At the end of the service he gave me one final hug. I had only been with him for a year, and I longed to stay with him, but that would have meant doing advanced work on the organ. My teacher had accepted by then that my lack of talent would have made that impossible. So, in deep sadness, I walked slowly out of the church.

At home that night, I thought about Mother again. I found it hard to blame her for anything; she and I were equally victims. Still, I felt she should have tried to prevent at least some of Father's excesses over the years. I thought of all the times she knew he was about to beat me. She could have taken my side then, but she chose not to. *Did she find strength in allying herself with him? Or was she as frightened of him as I was?*

There was nothing left for me at home. I had rebelled against both my parents in my mind and often in my words. Leaving now was not so much an act of rebellion as one of defeat.

I did not know where I would live, and I did not care. I knew I would stay in Melbourne for a short period. I needed to see

Mr. Rizzo again, just to experience that reassurance. His delight in seeing me on the few occasions I visited his church filled me with a rare sense of joy.

The night after I saw him for the last time, I fell asleep and began to dream that one day I would meet a man who would love my analytical mind and capacity to fight for justice. Hopefully he would also love my crazy sense of humor, together with my passionate nature.

Early next morning, I packed a suitcase and placed it in the hallway.

"Where do you think you're going?" Father yelled.

"I'm leaving. And this time I won't change my mind." He looked at me with contempt and walked to the back of the house as though he had no further interest in the matter.

"Goodbye, Mother," I said. She was crying. I wanted to reach out to her, but I felt as abandoned by her then as I had been in my cot.

Picking up my suitcase I walked to the front gate. As I turned to fasten the latch, I caught a glimpse of Mother at the window. In defiance, I grabbed my case and turned my back on her, intending to stride away without acknowledging her. To my surprise, I found my feet were barely moving. Did I want to leave her? Of course, I didn't. I would love to have taken her with me. We could both have been free. I felt had to reach out to her somehow. Once I was over the top of the hill, she would not be able to see me. But would she still be at the window? I wanted to look around, but what if she were not there? If she abandoned me this time, it would be what I deserved.

I looked up into the sky. Layers of thick cloud seemed to engulf me in their greyness. With a heavy sigh, I turned around. There was Mother. She had not moved. Slowly she raised her hand and put it on the glass. Tears filled my eyes; she loved me after all. I put my hand up and waved weakly. I loved her, and I always would.

I did not realize it at the time, but I was not only leaving my family and everything with which I was familiar; I was also about to enter a new and exciting phase of my life.

CHAPTER 25

Emancipation

After leaving home in a kind of daze, I managed to find a place to live in a church hostel. It was an old building with high ceilings and was not well maintained; the paint was peeling off the walls. Most of the rooms had two beds, but I managed to get a single room in a walled-off section of the verandah. The other residents were university students, and although they seemed friendly, I had little in common with them.

I felt terribly alone and wondered if God saw me as a failure. After all, I had rejected his representative in the family—my cruel father. At the same time, however, I was elated at never being subjected to cruel punishments or made to feel unworthy again. For the first time in my life, I could be who I wanted to be.

My plan was to spend one year in New Zealand. Memories of the childhood book I'd been given about the Inuit had left me longing to be in a snowy country. When I first saw pictures of the South Island of New Zealand, I knew that I would visit there one day. I had no job to go to but felt confident that my secretarial skills would be enough to make me employable.

I soon found myself in a travel agency, admiring enormous pictures of that spectacular scenery placed strategically around the walls. I first decided to do a little sightseeing, so the friendly agent mapped out an itinerary where I would fly to Wellington and then to Christchurch.

New Zealand was everything I could have hoped for—and even more. In Christchurch, I was allowed to climb up to the highest point inside the Anglican Cathedral, bringing back memories of the exciting times I'd had in the organ loft in Melbourne. A bus trip took me to the majestic Mt. Cook in the Southern Alps, which covers the length of the South Island. As the highest mountain in New Zealand, Mt. Cook is always covered in snow and is surrounded by massive glaciers and deep lakes.

The other highlight of my trip was Milford Sound with its towering peak, described by Rudyard Kipling as "the Eighth Wonder of the World." The scenic route to the Sound presented a fascinating display of snow-capped peaks, waterfalls, and layers of lush green growth. Taking a cruise around the Sound, I was delighted to see fur seals sunning themselves on the rocks and a pod of dolphins at play.

At the end of my short vacation, I went to Auckland on the North Island. The largest city in New Zealand, Auckland has a magnificent harbor. I soon found a secretarial position in a telecommunications company in the central business district, conveniently situated opposite the church hostel where I stayed. Prayers were the order of the day there and residents were expected to embrace the Christian faith. This was no problem for me, but again, I compared myself unfavorably with these young believers who seemed to have their faith all worked out. I also became an assistant church organist in a nearby suburb. The people everywhere were so friendly, but studying was my main focus. I was determined to go against my parent's ruling that I must not continue my education. They had prevented me from studying to become a teacher.

Before going to New Zealand, I discovered that the Australian National University in Canberra had a scheme whereby a mature age student who had completed three subjects at Higher School Certificate level could be given a provisional adult matriculation. Admission to an Arts degree required that one of those subjects be a language. As I had previously struggled through two years of French, I took the textbooks with me and tried to saturate myself in a language that was pleasing to a musical ear, but horribly difficult with its rules on the subjunctive mood.

My year in New Zealand was most enjoyable. I managed to visit various churches with a strong musical tradition. The hospitality I received from congregation members in the church I attended filled me with gratitude. I was also fortunate enough to be appointed secretary to a man who seemed to appreciate me as a person.

Following my plan, I moved to Canberra at the end of the year and lived in a government hostel. It was full of public servants who were not particularly friendly. But this did not concern me as my only reason for being there was to study.

Next to the hostel was a Lutheran church, where I joined the choir and played for some services. And at 24, I managed to pass English, History, and the dreaded French at the evening college run by the local High school. I also began my Arts degree but soon realized that I was not the arty type when it came to literature. One of my subjects was British History, which caused me no problems, but I fell flat on my face with advanced English, barely getting fifty percent for my assignments. This meant the sad end of my hopes of being a teacher, so I decided to move to Sydney.

During these years, I never experienced anything like a social life. I had always been an introvert and was more interested in thinking about challenging questions than in talking to people about matters that seemed inconsequential. As a result, I had few friends, and men were not interested in me. Having been rejected by my father, I think I carried a deeply held belief that I would never be attractive

175

to any man. I also felt that I had experienced deep psychological damage because of my painful upbringing. This view of myself led me to try various forms of therapy for two years, but none of them seemed to help. On one occasion, a therapist suggested that I gave the impression of not needing anything from anybody—including men.

Some of the treatment I had received involved counselling in groups. These consisted of people with a wide range of views, most of which did not involve a commitment to a particular religion. What surprised me was that many participants exhibited qualities similar to those listed in the New Testament as indicating a relationship with God through the saving work of Christ. This is described as a process of transformation—where the individual demonstrates love towards others, and experiences an attitude of peace and acceptance of whatever life offers. I had difficulty believing there was some fundamental difference between these qualities as shown by some of the believers I knew, and those in the therapy groups who saw no need to believe in a divine power. This led me to explore whether there could be a life-transforming dimension to our lives that is not dependent on the ideas we may accept at a conscious level.

At about that time, I was appointed organist and choir director in an Anglican church, a position I held for twelve years. The church had no children's choir, so I obtained permission from the Rector and the local primary school principal to conduct auditions with children in grades 4 to 6. Those who failed the audition were returned to their classrooms, while those who passed were given a pamphlet outlining the benefits of joining the church choir. These included outings such as ice skating and horse riding and an annual camp. The children had their own practice time, and as they grew older, they graduated to the adult choir, which eventually reached a very high standard.

The highlights of each year were a service of music on Palm Sunday and a service of Lessons and Carols the Sunday before Christmas. For the latter, I originally wanted to have the choir processing along the aisle with candles, but I was told that this could not be allowed as candles were deemed to be "high church." After each service, I was so elated I could hardly sleep. However, although I felt I had made a worthwhile contribution to the congregation's spiritual life, the experiences did nothing to convince me that I, myself, was a spiritual beneficiary. I would have stayed in my position had it not been for a weekend away attended by the most devout members of the church. I did not fall into that category, so I chose not to attend. Afterwards, it was conveyed to me that many people felt I had made the choir "elitist" and that because of this, I should resign. I did not want to exacerbate the division that I had obviously created within the congregation, so I left with deep sadness.

CHAPTER 26

Marriage, and a
Theological Debate

During my time at the Anglican church, a friend introduced me to Andrew Renoir. Tall and good looking, Andrew had a middle management position in the Public Service. Being an excellent soccer player, he had set up a football competition for public servants, which he organized in four divisions. Andrew was also keenly interested in music, particularly the work of Richard Wagner, and he owned five versions of that composer's Ring Cycle. Andrew was a good conversationalist with a broad general knowledge, and I learned a great deal from him. After dating for several years, we married when I was 36.

Although I had walked out of my family when I was twenty-three, I managed to maintain formal contact with my parents and my sisters, who had also left home as soon as possible. They understood how badly I had been treated and were sympathetic to what I had endured. I chose never to confront my father with what he had done, so the whole family were able to come to the wedding.

I fulfilled my basic obligations as a daughter for the remainder of my parents' lives. But I never paid them a visit. Their rejection of me caused me to believe that seeing them again would just stir up old wounds. In any case, their attitudes toward everything in life did not change over the years. Father was full of pride in holding his church position until his retirement.

Andrew proved to be an extraordinarily kind and generous husband, and our marriage lasted for thirty-five years until his death. From the beginning, we decided not to have children because of our dysfunctional backgrounds. Neither of us had received love from our own mothers, and I felt I would be incapable of being a loving mother to a child of my own.

Having fallen desperately in love with my organ teacher in Melbourne, I had been hoping that this would happen with Andrew. But instead, I found a different kind of love. I was drawn to Andrew's kindness and goodness and genuine care for me. To my surprise, our sex life was deeply satisfying, and I believe this was an essential reason for the stability of our relationship. I sometimes wondered what it would have been like to have a father as kind as Andrew.

Although he had not experienced a religious upbringing, I felt Andrew had a longing for something more in his life. He always accompanied me to church, though we never discussed questions of faith. I might have raised these matters with him had I not felt such a failure as a believer. On our honeymoon, we stayed at a seaside resort, and on the first Sunday, we attended the local Anglican church.

It was a charismatic service, where members of the congregation felt free to express their faith through bodily movements and unrestrained vocal expression. These people believe that following the experience of conversion, where a person accepts God's gift of salvation in Christ, a further blessing will occur when that individual receives the Holy Spirit. Through this experience, the person will discover a gift given by the Spirit, such as speaking in an unknown language or healing the sick. This claim is based on an account in the Bible where the Holy Spirit was said to have come upon a group of believers that gathered together several weeks after the death of Christ. This resulted in an ability to exercise a wide range of gifts.

In the situation today, no explanation is provided as to why most believers do not have such experiences. Perhaps it is believed that they don't ask for it, or if they do, they are at some deep level resisting the power of the Spirit.

It seemed to me that some of the charismatic people I knew had found something worthwhile in their lives. So at the end of the service, when the Rector invited people to come forward and receive the promised gift, Andrew and I responded. Although we were spoken to kindly and prayed for afterwards, the entire experience for me represented yet another spiritual dead end, while Andrew made no comment.

A few years later, I decided to make one last attempt to find what was missing in my spiritual life. I went to an interdenominational charismatic church with a large congregation, and joined about twenty others when the customary appeal was made. We were invited up onto the platform, where we formed a semicircle. I noticed that behind each person was someone from the congregation who had obviously been assigned a particular role.

The preacher had referenced the importance of receiving the Spirit, which was believed to occur when a hand is placed on the head of the recipient. Fortunately, I was in the middle of the row, which meant I could observe what happened when each person received this spiritual ministry. Everyone who was touched instantly fell backwards into the arms of the person behind. So as not to look obvious, or to suggest to the onlookers that I was somehow resisting the power of the Spirit, I dutifully fell in the prescribed manner. Having overcome the guilt of deceiving the preacher and the congregation, I concluded that either I was not "spiritual" enough to receive the gift, or this wasn't the path for me to find what was lacking in my life. All the same, I could not help wondering why some people were able to access a dimension of spiritual reality that seemed closed to me.

Early in our marriage, I completed a training course as a telephone counselor. This involved giving a sympathetic ear to people who were facing various problems. Counselors were not expected to provide solutions but to empathize with the feelings being expressed. One client had contacted me on several occasions and suggested that I train as a massage therapist. Such a thought had never occurred to me, but I found it intriguing and followed it up. After completing six months' training, I set up a business in our home, which ran for eleven years. Most of my patients were business or professional men. Although some had muscular problems, most worked under tremendous stress and just wanted a place to unwind. At the time, it seemed that if they had enjoyed a caring relationship with a loving and supportive partner, they would not have felt the need to pay a stranger to provide what could only ever be a substitute.

Several years after I began my practice, I met a woman who suggested that I apply for admission to a one-year postgraduate degree in Psychology. When I learned that the course did not require a student to have an undergraduate degree, I became quite excited. In my application, I submitted an article I had written when I was in my late 30s, which had been published in an Australian Anglican journal. This article had critiqued the work of an American psychologist, Lawrence Crabb, who claimed that all psychological problems could be resolved through Christian faith. Crabb argued that all you must do is believe that God loves you, and your need for love will be met. Moreover, you must believe that God will meet your needs for human love because he will send people who will give you that love into your life.

When I read Crabb's work, I became very angry. Crabb seemed to be implying that if a person with psychological problems was not healed after applying his methods, they would not only be left with their original condition but also would have to bear a heavy spiritual burden. As far as I was concerned, this was an insupportable position, so I decided to write an article critiquing such ideas. Contrary to Crabb's argument, I suggested that God's love can never make up for the absence of love from other human beings. Furthermore, because of human sinfulness, there is no guarantee that we will always receive love.

A short time later and quite by accident, I met Michael, the head of the Anglican Counselling Service in Sydney. I wasted no time in taking advantage of the coincidence by asking him straight out, "What do you think of Lawrence Crabb?"

Michael hesitated. "Well… er, people have different views…"

"Well, I think Lawrence Crabb is dangerous," I declared. At that point, I was not too worried about Michael's view of the author. But when I saw his eyes light up, I knew I had found a kindred spirit.

So I continued. "The way I see it, the Bible does not address the question of psychological healing or the damage that can be done to us in our earliest years. It is concerned only with the behavior over which we have conscious control and for which we can be held morally responsible."

Michael had serious reservations about what he described as Crabb's cognitive behaviorist approach. This way of thinking had been enthusiastically embraced by the clergy in Sydney, many of whom, like my father, take every word of the Bible literally. Michael continued, "Their overriding concern is that their congregations simply believe the facts, so they just swallow everything Crabb says—hook, line and sinker."

Although Michael and I agreed about the problem with Crabb's psychological theory, we disagreed on how he addresses the question of love.

"In Crabb's theory," I suggested, "because we have the love of God, that's all any of us need to feel loved. But in my view, that's not enough," I referred to C.S. Lewis's book, *The Four Loves,* where he distinguishes between what he calls "gift love" and "need loves." The latter include friendship and eros, which I described as "selective loves" in my article. I suggested to Michael that God created us with a psychological need for friendship and eros, and if we don't have that, it cannot be compensated for merely by knowing that God loves us.

After considering my argument for a while, Michael said, "I can't help feeling somehow that you are wrong." He then took a quick glance at his watch, "Look, I have to run. I'm due to give a lecture at Macquarie University," which was half an hour's drive away.

Determined to convince him, I made a snap decision. "I'm coming with you," I announced, having no idea how I would get back. That didn't matter because I'd found someone intelligent with whom I could have a rewarding and stimulating debate. We went back and forth, arguing our points throughout the entire drive. Then just as we were entering the University gates, Michael said, "Yes, I believe you're right." I could hardly describe the sense of relief I experienced at that moment.

After my article was published, as we had predicted, the Sydney clergy came down on me like a ton of bricks. But I would not admit defeat, so Michael and I got together and wrote a rebuttal. This received the same kind of comments as the original article, where the writers tried all they could to rescue Crabb. We wrote a further response, but since the replies added nothing to the arguments they had already advanced, we decided not to pursue it.

CHAPTER 27

Giving a Voice to
Abused Men

My article about Crabb came in very handy when applying for the post-graduate Psychology course a few years later. Submitting it along with my piano and organ diplomas was sufficient to gain me admission to the course. All proceeded well, and then at the end of the first year something entirely unexpected and completely unprecedented altered my life's trajectory. The university authorities decided to give us credit at Master's level for the year we had just completed. I was delighted to have completed the first part of a degree, and with the encouraging comments of my examiners, I felt confident that I could complete the course. Andrew was so pleased that I had been given this opportunity.

During the following year, we were required to write a thesis related to our own life experiences, and I decided to bring together two aspects of my life. One was the abuse I had suffered at the hands of my father. The other drew on some of the abuse stories I'd heard from men in my work, both as a telephone counselor and a massage therapist treating male patients with muscular problems. Having seen the pain in these men's faces and feeling the tension in their bodies, some of them slowly began to open up. They told me about the women in their lives who were treating them in ways that negated their sense of self and seriously affected their ability to function. I had no idea that the abuse of men by their female partners was—and sadly still is—a serious social problem that is largely unacknowledged by society. It has the effect of exacerbating a sense of disempowerment that many men experience today.

Researching the literature in this field, I discovered that studies of male victims investigate mainly physical abuse. In contrast, those relating to the abuse of women cover physical, sexual and psychological abuse. I'd been privy to some very painful confessions. So I decided to carry out a similar wide-ranging enquiry about men and to focus my thesis on physical, psychological and sexual abuse.

I contacted the editor of a men's magazine held in the State Library of New South Wales, who provided names of various organizations that conducted groups for men. These fell into two categories: support groups, where men shared their experiences in an environment of trust, and groups that were open to the public (including women), that worked towards reforming the law and public policy. I forwarded to the conveners of both groups an information sheet about my research. They then circulated this to members of the groups either by post, email or in group meetings. I was invited to address meetings of the groups working for reform.

Included on the sheet was an invitation for men who had experienced abuse to be participants in the research project and phone me to arrange an interview. The limitations I imposed were that the abuse period had been at least twelve months and that the relationship had ended by then. I did not want to include men whose sense of empowerment was such that they ended the relationship after the first abusive episode. Also, I wanted to avoid creating additional emotional stress on men who were still living with their abusers.

Through unstructured interviews, I asked the men to tell me their stories, with particular reference to their feelings about the incidents. I interviewed 48 men from Australia and New Zealand, some face-to-face and others over the phone.

My goal was to explore the nature and extent of abuse against men, how it affected them, and the social structures that enabled the abuse to occur. My hypotheses were that the pain men experience as victims of female abuse is of such a magnitude that they often cannot bear it; also, that there is widespread prejudice against men, which works against a just resolution in situations of heterosexual conflict.

In choosing to conduct unstructured interviews, I sought to enter the participants' worlds as deeply as possible. As I had been a victim of male abuse, I felt I could empathize deeply with the pain and loss of self-respect that an abused person experiences. I found myself resonating with the participants' feelings of shame, anger and betrayal.

Since the men I interviewed had suffered abuse by a woman, my role as a female researcher was ambivalent. I found myself wanting to give the men the kind of empathy they had not received from their partners. I also wanted them to know that I understood the shattering effects of abuse due to my own experience. In the early interviews, I disclosed what I had suffered at the hands of a man. But I later discontinued the disclosure because it might have influenced how the participants presented their material. I did not want them to think I held negative attitudes towards men. Or, worse still, that they could see me as a radical feminist in disguise who might use the information against them.

An assumption I brought to the research process was that the abused person must be given a voice. In my own experience, while I was "under the roof" of the abuser, I'd had no rights. Had I told anyone what was happening, I would have either been disbelieved or told to be submissive. It seemed that abused men are silenced the way I was, or if they do speak, they are not heard.

I decided not to ask any of the men whether their behavior might have contributed to the abuse. Since men in this situation are continually being blamed for their predicament, I felt that such an approach would have been disempowering. There were one or two occasions when I felt there might have been some contributing factors to the abuse. But I was surprised that several men blamed themselves for behaviors that I felt were perfectly normal and acceptable. This is consistent with the attitude of those men in society who carry deep collective guilt toward all women.

Many participants were well educated and had sought to work through their personal issues, either with a therapist or in support groups. After listening to these stories, I found it difficult to believe that women could act in this way. Physical abuse included injuring the man by throwing heavy objects, stabbing, burning, or smashing glass objects across his face. The men must have worried about not being believed because they would offer to show me medical reports to validate their accounts.

Psychological abuse cases involved women claiming to have had affairs throughout the marriage, ridiculing the man's body, intelligence, and ability to function, or denigrating him in front of others. Sexual abuse included withholding sex as a form of punishment or using it as a means of manipulation. Some women had a need to control and humiliate their partners by demanding sex at any time. If the man did not comply, they would go on the attack. Retaliation included emotional blackmail, locking the man out of the house, or making disparaging comments that he had failed the test of manhood. Women would often devise "punishments" for their partners. These included disappearing from the house without explanation, sleeping in the spare room, treating their partner "like a boarder," making him do all the work in the house, not passing on messages, and not communicating with him at all. Inappropriate and improper misuse of money placed many men in difficult situations.

One common method employed by abusive women was to place the man in a situation where whatever he did was wrong, even when he gave in to all of their demands. A woman can maintain total power over a man by making threats involving his safety and wellbeing or that of the children. The worst forms of abuse men reported were the sense of powerlessness they felt when their children were being abused or used as weapons against them. Many men felt undermined, particularly in their relationships with their children.

At times the men seemed to experience a kind of enrichment from telling their stories. Some of them could not get to the end without tears in their eyes. Many of the participants in the study came to believe that the abuse was all their fault. In their experiences of disempowerment, judgment, and identity violation, the men expressed various emotions. But the most poignant and distressing to me as a researcher was their sense of hopelessness and betrayal.

My study aimed to enter into the experiences of abused men and alert society to the pain they are enduring. In telling these men that I would publish their stories, I felt I was giving them some faint hope that the world could become a better place. I suggested that many people now believe what they are saying and will do everything they can to bring that knowledge to the broader community.

It seemed that the ability to abuse another person can arise from serious deficiencies in an abuser's upbringing. My own father had been a victim of violence, but because he had persuaded himself that he was such a wonderful person, he probably believed that by beating me, he could cause me to become as admired as he was.

In giving abused men a voice and the opportunity to tell their stories in an atmosphere of trust, I went on a journey of discovery. As an abused person, I was giving myself a voice. The men's pain became my pain. Their injustice was my injustice, their anger, my own anger. And so I listened to myself as I listened to them, and in helping to free them, I began to free myself.

It seemed that the ability to enter another person's pain can be mutually healing. But that ability, as far as I was concerned, was seriously lacking in my father, despite his view that in humiliating me, he was carrying out the will of God. Although in my own mind I had tried to separate my father's behavior from what I believed God would have wanted from a parent, I could not help feeling that perhaps I deserved at least some of his treatment.

My view that I was a failure as a believer was undoubtedly due to the damage caused by my upbringing and was related to a deep-seated fear that there could be something spiritually wrong with me. But then I had an unexpected experience that challenged my thinking and took me in an entirely different direction.

CHAPTER 28

A Life-Changing Experience

I was fifty years old and Andrew and I had been married for fourteen harmonious years. Life had settled down into a comfortable routine when suddenly, out of the blue, something remarkable happened that I was so ill-equipped to understand, I almost lost my mind.

I awoke one day with only two tasks on my schedule: to clip around the edges of the lawn and to clean the car. I placed the cleaning equipment along with my car keys in the middle of the lawn. When I had finished clipping the grass and was ready to move on to my next task, I was dumbfounded to find that my car keys had disappeared. The car cleaning equipment was still where I left it, but the keys were nowhere in sight. Where could they have gone? It would have been impossible for anybody to steal them. With one hand shielding my eyes from the sun, I looked across the lawn, wondering if I had unwittingly kicked them over to a different area. There was no sign of them. I retraced my steps back to the house, assuming that I must have just imagined leaving them on the grass, and convinced I would find them on the kitchen counter. They were not there.

It was a surreal situation. A set of keys cannot disappear into thin air. I'd never encountered anything like this before, and it affected me deeply. I was an intelligent, rational person who viewed the world as a predominantly orderly place. But this was neither rational nor orderly. I was so challenged by the situation that I experienced a kind of breakdown.

My thoughts were just consumed by what had happened. For several days, all I could do was to walk through every room, out into the yard and around and around the lawn, and back into the house again. No matter how many times I repeated the exercise, I still could not come to terms with it. It was as though I had been thrown into an alien universe where the laws of the only universe I had ever known had just ceased to be. I felt almost as if I no longer existed. This was when I realized that I was in serious trouble.

I have to find out what happened to those keys, I kept telling myself. So I did something that I would never have contemplated before: I made an appointment to see a psychic. From time to time I had heard psychics speaking to people on the radio, and they seemed able to convey accurate information.

My first thought was to look in the phone book, and I was pleased to discover that there was a psychic who had a practice in a nearby suburb. After making an appointment, I walked with some trepidation up the front steps, wondering what the session would be like. I had heard that some clients are more difficult to "read" than others. And given my unusual personality, I felt sure that I would be in the group that caused problems!

An elderly man greeted me warmly at the door and led me into a quiet, darkened room. After a few minutes of silence, he asked me how he could help. I told him about the disappearance of the keys and the days of desperation that followed. Eventually, he said, "I can't see what's happened to your keys, but I don't think you'll ever find them," (which turned out to be the case). I was deflated. But then he said something that to me was almost incomprehensible.

"There's a being on the other side who wants to talk to you. I see her in a wartime nurse's uniform. I'm being given her first name, which is Edith. The second name starts with either a C or a K."

"Oh …" I said, a bit nonplussed, wondering who it could be. I wracked my brains trying to think *Who is Edith C or Edith K?* Then an idea struck. "Would that be Edith Cavell?" I asked hesitantly, not understanding what this could mean.

"Yes." The psychic confirmed. "That's the name I'm being given." The expression on his face conveyed that he had no idea that Edith Cavell was a famous British nurse. Her strong religious beliefs led to her saving soldiers' lives from both sides without discrimination during the First World War. Unfairly court-martialed and sentenced to death for helping some 200 Allied soldiers escape from German-occupied Belgium, Cavell's execution by a German firing squad had received worldwide condemnation and extensive press coverage. That the psychic seemed to have no knowledge of her seemed like a good sign to me.

Then things got even stranger.

"You own a pendant," Edith declared through the psychic. She then described it accurately to me.

"When you get home," she continued, "I want you to hold that pendant perfectly still and ask a question. If the answer is 'yes,' it will swing one way, and if the answer is 'no,' it will swing the other way."

Being a skeptic by disposition, I quietly assured myself there was no way in the world this would work. Still, the moment I arrived home, I closed all the doors and windows so there would be no breeze, and I held that pendant rigid. Cautiously, I asked it a question. I could hardly believe it when the thing actually moved! I sat for a while, my mind weaving back and forth between stark astonishment and a barely stifled excitement at the ramifications of what this meant. The thought that I could actually communicate with someone who had no physical presence in the world I occupied was mind-boggling. *Was this real? Or was I somehow moving the pendant without realizing it?* With my left hand gripped tightly around my wrist to keep it perfectly steady, I continued asking questions, testing the pendant repeatedly. Eventually, I had to concede that it wasn't my imagination. Some other mechanism, energy, or spirit could control the pendant to communicate intelligently with me. It seemed like a miracle. But the more I thought about it, the more I realized it was no more extraordinary than many of the "miracle" stories I'd read in the Bible.

Although contact with psychics was regarded as contrary to Christian teaching, I recalled that in the Hebrew scriptures, King Saul contacted the witch of Endor, who could summon the spirit of the prophet Samuel. After complaining about being disturbed from his rest, Samuel made an accurate prediction about the downfall of Saul. Thinking about this incident gave me confidence that communicating with individuals in spirit was a legitimate (if somewhat strange) activity with many precedents, and that I should continue along this path. Once I accepted the fact, it didn't take long to recognize the pendant's pattern—it swung horizontally for 'yes' and vertically for 'no.' At that point, Edith confirmed that she would guide me on my new journey.

Having developed the view that I was a failure as a believer, I'd come to feel that if there was a God, he wasn't interested in any contact with me. But now that a being on the other side had reached out to me, I no longer felt that I was spiritually alone or that I had been abandoned.

At that time, I was studying for my Psychology degree, and most of the questions I asked Edith concerned the ideas of Carl Jung. For example, I would ask her, "Can we always discover our shadow side?" And, "Did Jung believe in a personal God?" As these questions are debated by scholars, it was of great value to me to receive Edith's responses. I would contact her a few times each day. On one occasion, I was surprised when instead of moving vertically or horizontally, the pendant spun round in a circle. I eventually worked out that some questions could not be answered with a simple "yes" or "no." And when this happened, I would have to rephrase questions so they could be answered in the usual way.

On important matters, I would write down the answers. But from the beginning, I never doubted that the information I was being given was correct. It did not seem possible that there could be any other conceivable reason for a pendant to move of its own accord.

After several months of contact with Edith, one day the pendant suddenly stopped responding to me. This immediately put me into a state of panic. At first I had a strong feeling—and I don't know where it came from—that Edith was ending her contact with me, but that someone else would carry on the work. When I asked her if this was the case, I was relieved when the pendant responded affirmatively. I then had to go through all the letters of the alphabet to find out who the new guide was. The name was Aristotle.

This can't be true, I thought. *Why would a famous philosopher want to talk to a nonentity like me?* I was so freaked out about this that I went to see another psychic. I didn't tell her anything about myself, but in the middle of the reading, she said, "I see a group of ancient Greek philosophers discussing your work."

Following this affirmation, I sat quietly in my lounge one day and, with great trepidation, asked if I was speaking to Aristotle. My joy was indescribable when the pendant moved horizontally. At first, it was difficult for me to work out what information Aristotle wanted to convey to me. But through a seemingly endless rephrasing of questions, I was told that after I had completed my Master's degree in Psychology, I should apply to do a PhD in philosophy. When my Master's thesis was subsequently awarded a high distinction, it confirmed Aristotle's message that I should continue with my studies.

Being able to connect with the spirit world was an important factor in helping me to understand the oneness of all reality. It seemed to me that those who have departed this life are merely undergoing a transition to a different way of being, in which the divisions we experience in our three-dimensional world simply disappear.

Although contact with beings in another dimension was critical in the concepts I was developing, I did not discuss my experience with anyone, including Andrew. If I had done, he and my friends and family would have had serious doubts about my sanity!

Looking back on the way things evolved, I realized that the reason I lost my keys was so that I could be introduced to these higher beings and their ideas. It was not as though the theory I eventually developed was ever revealed to me in detail, but each piece of information added to the growing picture.

CHAPTER 29

From Psychology
to Philosophy

It so happened that the lecturers in the psychology course were
fascinated by the German philosopher, Martin Heidegger. They
frequently quoted from his major work, *Being and Time*. So, I read
the book... once... twice ... and even a third time. But I could not
make any sense of it. What Heidegger said in that book was as un-
convincing to me as Lawrence Crabb's assertion that psychological
problems could be resolved through Christian experience.

Throughout my Master's course, and for two years after grad-
uating, I continued my massage practice. At the same time, I was
reading everything I could find on Heidegger, and soon formed a
view of where he had gone astray in his major work. He seemed to
be mistaken in using everyday events to support his primary claim
that there is some kind of background to our lives of which we are
unaware. Many scholars regard Heidegger as one of the twentieth
century's most significant philosophers, but as far as I was concerned,
this opinion was not warranted.

To complete a doctorate in philosophy, a student must have
completed an undergraduate degree in that field, preferably with
honors, or have obtained a Master's degree. The only reason I had the
courage to apply for entry into a doctoral program, having never been
to a philosophy lecture in my life, was that Aristotle had suggested I
should pursue philosophy at the highest level.

Following this advice, I approached the universities in Sydney. But they would not even consider me because of my lack of background in the discipline. I then contacted the University of Tasmania in Hobart, where the professor was a recognized authority on Heidegger. After listening to my reasons as to why his favorite philosopher was wrong, the professor simply said, "Oh, you'll be all right, just send in your application." He had obviously assumed that I had a degree in philosophy.

When I told Andrew that I was considering spending three years studying in Tasmania for a PhD, he received the idea with equanimity. Given how companionable our relationship was, I didn't think he would object too much. As I anticipated, he was very understanding and supportive, and I assured him that I would fly home once a year to be with him.

When my acceptance came through without any problems, I marveled at how easily everything seemed to have fallen into place. From regretting having had to resign from the roles I had enjoyed as organist and director of the choirs at my church, I now saw that situation as a blessing. Had I stayed there, I could never have undertaken tertiary studies.

Financially, everything seemed to be in my favor too. In those days, the government would give $25,000 to a university when a student submitted a doctoral thesis passed by two independent examiners. In addition to not having to pay for my tuition, the University of Tasmania actually viewed me as a potentially profitable asset! And thanks to having been a lifelong saver, I had sufficient funds to cover my accommodation and living expenses for the entire three years.

I couldn't help wondering what mysterious power had rearranged my life so that I had the freedom and the means to set this new agenda for myself. Regardless of who or what was responsible, I was grateful.

Arriving in Hobart in 2003, I found affordable living quarters in a converted garage. When winter arrived, it was freezing, but being resourceful, I used old sheets to create tents. One was placed over my bed, one over my computer desk, and one over the couch. I then placed heaters inside the tents. This way, I was able to survive three dark and frigid winters.

I didn't make any friends, and I never socialized or took time out for any kind of recreation—in fact, the only person I spoke to during the whole period was my supervisor. Since I had never studied philosophy, I had to learn as much as I could as quickly as possible. So I devoted every second of my waking life to reading, going to the library, and writing. The only sightseeing I did was when I took a week off at Andrew's insistence and drove to the north of the island, where I stayed in a caravan park near where the Tamar River meets the ocean. Tasmania is an exquisitely beautiful island, its only rival being the South Island of New Zealand.

Writing my PhD thesis meant that, initially, I was totally dependent on Aristotle for guidance. This was all the more important due to my lack of background in philosophy. Although I was confident in the accuracy of the information he gave me, the whole experience was at times overwhelming. Through my use of the pendant, Aristotle was able to help me clarify what the various commentators were saying. As had been the case when I was working with Edith, I had to frame my questions carefully to receive the information that I needed.

The more I engaged with these higher beings, the stronger and more dependable my intuition became. Before long, I understood what they wanted to share with me even before asking a question. The importance of this new skill I was developing became apparent to me one day when the pendant would not respond. Disappointed and curious to know why it had stopped working, I found myself formulating this question in my mind without really expecting to receive an answer.

But almost instantly, as if someone else was planting a seed, a strange thought popped into my head. *I no longer need the pendant because I can just as easily communicate with my guides using my hands!* Turning the idea over in my mind, I realized that it made a lot of sense; hand movements were faster. It also allowed me to ask questions even while driving or walking along the road. When I put it to the test and found it accurate, I felt a dizzying sense of satisfaction.

It seemed that mastering the pendant had been an initiation that unlocked a secret door to a more advanced level of communication. This method of contact with my spirit guides continues to serve me to the present day. It has not only been philosophers who have given me guidance, but other beings on a higher plane who have insights into the challenges of living in this rapidly changing world.

After several months, Aristotle handed me over to the recently deceased French philosopher, Jacques Derrida, who had disagreed with Heidegger's interpretation of a concept in Plato's thought. Finally, I was referred to the medieval theologian and philosopher Thomas Aquinas. He assisted me in my analysis of mysticism, where I argued that Heidegger could have become a mystic, but that he could not let go of the ideas I had challenged in his earlier writings.

One of the privileges of being a doctoral student is hiring and firing supervisors. So when the professor took extended leave and referred me to a lecturer who turned out to be a nightmare, I discontinued working with him. When the next one proved unsuitable, in desperation I sought Aristotle's advice. He told me to look on the university website, where I discovered just one lecturer who had written an article on Heidegger. I approached her in great trepidation and explained the problems I'd had.

"Would you be able to take me?" I pleaded.

"Of course," she said without hesitation, and she turned out to be the most fantastic supervisor. She gave me every encouragement and became a much-valued friend. However, owing to specific difficulties she was experiencing, she decided to accept a position at the University of Wollongong—a city just a short distance from Sydney.

So after three years in Hobart, I decided to return home to Andrew. It was so good to be with him again and experience his love, support and encouragement.

Because of my lack of background in philosophy, I needed an extra two years to complete the thesis, and in 2009, at the age of sixty-eight, I submitted the work. It received high praise from the two examiners. One of them described what I had written as "outstanding," and the other gave me a special commendation. By this time, both my parents had died, and I was relieved to know that I could never be condemned for having done something that, in their view, would have made me even more "aggressive." I could not help comparing my parents' view of me with the admiration and love that I received from my wonderful husband.

CHAPTER 30

Losing Andrew but Finding
Spiritual Freedom

Andrew was so proud that I had obtained a doctorate. I think he felt that his kindness had been rewarded in supporting my original move to Hobart. But sadly, his health began to deteriorate a few months after my return, and one day I found him collapsed unconscious on the kitchen floor. The ambulance soon arrived, but his prognosis was not good at the hospital. After several difficult months in rehabilitation, Andrew died peacefully in his sleep at the age of eighty. I was deeply grateful for the life we had shared. Without everything he had given me, I would never have been able to complete what I came to believe was my life's purpose.

The next several months I spent in deep mourning. Life without Andrew seemed so empty. But having a big gap in my life enabled me to spend time reflecting on my upbringing. My religious family had taught me to believe I was a sinner. And unless I accepted God's gift of salvation through the death of Christ, I would go to hell. I was also conditioned to believe that people who make this commitment will have their lives transformed through the indwelling power of the Holy Spirit. Because of that programming, I devoted the first fifty years of my life to the Christian faith, surrendering myself to God and what I believed was his will for my life.

But when I did not develop any of the qualities the Bible lists as evidence of this power, I began to see myself as a spiritual wasteland.

I had met people of various persuasions who were living examples of the qualities I lacked. Although I could see transformation in the lives of others, I couldn't see any trace of it in myself. To me, that could only mean that either I was a bigger sinner than everybody else, or I was doing something wrong. Whatever the case, I did not consider departing from the faith. Going to hell was not an option.

After leaving home, I tried for several decades to make my faith work, but in the end, I realized this would never happen. Receiving such a favorable response to my doctoral thesis encouraged me to try to uncover the mystery that had plagued me all my life. *Why was it that people with all sorts of beliefs—and those with none—exhibited qualities that I'd thought could only result from a vital relationship with the divine?*

I decided to look more closely at the various traditions—what they had in common and where they differed. So for the next several years, I devoted every waking moment to investigating these crucial questions. The deeper my investigation went, the more I realized that my research would have to encompass not only the fields of philosophy and psychology, but also mysticism and quantum theory.

In studying the origins of religion, it became clear that all religions are founded on the experiences of individuals who had gained insight into the nature of ultimate reality. They then formulated those ideas into systems of thought that attracted followers.

As I investigated further, it gradually dawned on me that the idea of the God I had been raised to accept had ceased to have any real meaning in my life. As I contemplated that radical change in my outlook, I came to a wonderfully liberating realization—*there is no God who sees me as a worthless sinner.*

As a result of my investigations, I wrote an academic book on this complex subject.* Since I am not alone in enduring such a rigorous upbringing, I felt that sharing my journey from religious indoctrination to spiritual freedom might help those who were similarly influenced to find a pathway to their own liberation.

Early in my research, I realized that some of the most critical questions ever asked concern how everything we know came into being and how this process or event relates to the purposes of our existence.

We live in a three-dimensional world, so we see ourselves as separate from each other and from all reality. Research in various fields suggests, however, that we are all one. This being the case, our conscious view of our separateness can conflict with a deeper sense of that oneness. If we become aware of this feeling, we may seek ways of restoring that fundamental connectedness. One of those ways involves believing that there must be a God who can save us from a situation that we feel is somehow our fault. Based on this assumption, religions have come into being that attempt to teach us to acknowledge our failure and reach out to the one who can restore us and make us whole. However, it is believed that this wholeness is only partial because there is still a separation between ourselves and this God.

---

*   *God Interrogated: Reinterpreting the Divine* will be published by John Hunt
    Publishing in Spring 2023 and will be available in bookstores and online.
    A brief summary of the information I uncovered during those years of inquiry
    is included here as an Appendix. Subjects include the emergence of religion,
    why people believe in God, philosophical and scientific approaches to the
    question of the divine, together with discussions on Gnosticism, Mysticism
    and Quantum Theory.

Three major religious traditions known as monotheisms attribute the whole of reality to a divine, all-powerful Creator. The earliest, Judaism, holds that God revealed himself to the Israelites and declared that if they obey his laws, he will acknowledge them as the people chosen to bring his light to the world.

Christianity teaches that God came to earth in the form of his son, Jesus of Nazareth. And while our relationship with him has been broken because of our sinfulness and rebellion against God, it can be restored through faith in the saving death and resurrection of Jesus.

Within Islam, the name of the one true God is Allah, and the Quran is his most perfect revelation. To Muslims, Muhammad is the final prophet sent by Allah to teach human beings how to live.

With regard to Christianity, the various acts of divine inspiration involved numerous people over lengthy periods, each presenting different perspectives and interpretations of the sacred texts based on their personal life experiences. Consequently, we now have multiple groups with varying approaches to the teachings as a whole and different degrees of liberty allowed for interpreting specific aspects of the faith. At one end of the scale, we have the most prominent Christian body—the Roman Catholic Church—which has stringent limits on the acceptability of an individual's insight into truth. At the opposite end are Protestant groups that respect the autonomy of a person's relationship with God.

For most of my life I believed in a God of love. But as an infant in my cot, I developed a sense that whatever existed was hostile to me. By the time I was a young adult, it had been beaten into me that the problem was entirely mine. Something was wrong with *me*. I wasn't good enough or obedient enough to please God. This caused me to believe that I was unlovable. Apart from the slight doubt cast on this opinion when my organ teacher seemingly found something to admire in me, the belief that I wasn't deserving of love had formed part of my identity.

The hardest thing for me to understand in my Christian upbringing was the idea that God was "all good." If that were true, I wondered how people with religious beliefs who behave cruelly to others could absolve their behavior by attributing it to "God's will." This question became relevant when considering the behavior of my father. I wondered whether he had been misguided or ignorant in his perception of God, or if there could be some other explanation.

Through my studies, I learned that many forms of psychological abuse in an individual's early years can adversely affect subsequent behavior. As a result, some people who become parents cannot love their children; even though they may provide everything for them, they're just incapable of love. And anyone who grows up with an inadequate sense of self because of serious failures in parenting is highly vulnerable to external influences. This is particularly the case with systems of belief that these people sense will somehow compensate them for their lack of self-worth. My father's terrible family background had left him severely psychologically damaged and robbed him of the ability to control his behavior or to love his own child. But he had religion. The only way he could feel worthwhile was to convince himself that God loved him.

I could never work out whether my father's cruelty could be totally attributed to his appalling upbringing. It has been suggested that his treatment of me represented a serious moral failure. But whatever the case, I came to the view that it was in my interests to forgive him. Not doing so would have been detrimental to my own growth.

My research showed there are many paths to fulfillment and to experiencing a sense of connection to that elusive mystery that gives us the sense that we are not alone. We may call that mystery God, Allah, Brahman, the Universe, consciousness, or all that is. I concluded that people can experience that oneness either by embracing one of the monotheisms, following a philosophy with no concept of a personal God, or adopting a secular approach. My view is that this oneness underlies all systems of thought that seek to explain the meaning of our existence. It would also seem that because of this intrinsic connectedness, there is a part of us, hidden deep within our being, that carries the potential for connecting with that oneness.

Although challenges to the idea of a personal God are considerable, in the end, the question is fundamentally one of transformation—a feeling of being whole. When it comes to finding this personal fulfillment, factual knowledge that sustains us at the level of our three-dimensional existence proves inadequate.

The deep-seated need to attain that goal can lead us in many directions. Should we find that our innermost needs are met through belief in a divine being, we may still hold to the idea that a gulf exists between ourselves and the Creator because of our sin. On the other hand, the depth of our experience can indicate that a fundamental connectedness is occurring here, as indicated in the words of St. Paul, "Who can separate us from the love of God?"

The alternative view is that because of the oneness of all reality, any sense that, as humans, we are distinct and separate from others, can be resolved through the awareness that each of us is a unique expression of that ultimate mystery. This oneness has been experienced by mystics, and is confirmed through quantum discoveries.

As a sufferer of physical and psychological abuse, I spent several decades endeavoring to live by the tenets of the faith in which I had been raised. Through all those years, I yearned for the kind of connection that would result in the same transformation I had witnessed in the lives of others. I tried everything to make my beliefs work. But still, despite my failure to achieve this, a seed buried deep within me would not allow me to give up that quest for wholeness.

Understanding that, ultimately, I am one with the whole of reality has enabled me to develop the most important quality of all—a love for other people. Such a transformation in my life is based on the recognition that we are all integral to that oneness, and each of us is adding to the experience of the universe. Also involved here is an acceptance of the circumstances in which we find ourselves, knowing that they are designed to fulfill a purpose that may at present be hidden from us.

The way I was raised prevented me from fulfilling my potential as a human being. My father and mother had a fixed idea of what this potential was all about. It was governed by what they read in the Bible about how females should behave. The result was that I was constrained, unable to follow my passion for knowledge— unless it was expressed in terms allowed by their narrow, rigid beliefs. Although at first I could not seek my own path, my longing to understand the reason for my existence finally enabled me to break free and find what would transform my life.

The realization of the oneness of all reality has been with me for many years, guiding me through the challenges of daily living and giving me peace and serenity.

And I encourage you to find your own path. It may involve following unexpected signs such as a book about spirituality that mysteriously comes into your possession, or a movie that stirs the deepest part of your being. If things don't work out at first, be assured that you are being led to some greater reality that will eventually enrich your life beyond measure.

Just as I found an answer to my deepest yearnings, I trust that you, too, will find a path that fills your life with meaning and fulfilment.

Appendix

To understand why some believers experience transformation while others don't, I became interested in studying how philosophers have addressed the question of God. I was surprised at how widely their opinions varied regarding how we can discover whether or not he actually exists, what he may be like, and the kind of relationship we may have with him.

Why do people believe in God?

There are many reasons why people believe in a divine being. These include: a sense that a higher power must be responsible for everything that exists; an intuitive feeling that there is something more to life than can be explained by what is immediately apparent; confidence in the reported experiences of others, particularly those historical figures whose teachings formed the basis of the various belief systems. The decision may also result from perceived deficiencies in an individual's life experience. Among the needs that could be met in this context would be a sense of having sins forgiven, receiving divine love, guidance, and protection, and finding meaning and purpose in life.

Although we cannot prove God's existence, anyone who believes in him would expect to see some evidence of transformation resulting from their faith. However, a person can accept a given belief system's doctrines and practice the behaviors it requires without experiencing any deep-seated sense of inner change. Conversely, if such an awareness should become a reality, the individual would have reason to consider the experience as confirming the teachings embraced.

One factor working against the validation of beliefs by personal experience is that similar kinds of transformation can occur in the lives of people who follow the different traditions. Although there are commonalities in what the monotheisms teach, many of their ideas are contradictory or inconsistent. What is considered true in one belief system may be regarded as false in another. For example, the Christian doctrine that God became man in the person of Jesus is refuted in Judaism and Islam, where the very idea of an incarnated God is considered blasphemous.

Varieties in Religious Beliefs

Those who have embraced a particular faith regard their belief to be true. People who fail to experience any profound change by devoting themselves to their religion will still cling to their belief because it must be true if their God said it. They rely on their own reasoning processes to conclude that they have both found the correct God and understand what he requires of them. Nevertheless, this faith in their ability to reason cannot account for the absence of transformation in their own lives or its presence in the lives of those who hold opposing views.

Within Christianity, the various acts of divine inspiration involved numerous people over lengthy periods, each presenting different perspectives and interpretations of the sacred texts based on their own life experiences.

Consequently, we now have multiple groups with varying approaches to the teachings, and different degrees of liberty allowed for interpreting specific aspects of the faith. For example, at one end of the scale, we have the largest Christian body—the Roman Catholic Church—which has stringent limits on the acceptability of an individual's insight into truth. At the opposite end are Protestant groups that respect the autonomy of a person's relationship with God.

The philosophical approach

Unlike science, which questions factual accuracy through the formulation and testing of hypotheses, philosophy examines all forms of human knowledge and experience, including the possibility of rational justification for belief in the existence of God. Issues discussed in philosophy relating to God's existence include the nature of reality and how we can know anything at all—i.e., whether we rely on our reason, the evidence of our senses, or our inner experience.

Philosophy began in the West with thinkers in Ancient Greece, where myths explained everything in the human experience. Gods and goddesses were regarded as the personification of impersonal forces who exerted power over the world. They were believed to protect and guide their inhabitants if appropriate ceremonies and sacrifices were offered. That changed around the 7th century BC. When the Greeks recognized that earlier religious ideas were merely products of artistic imagination, they began to replace the world of myth with an approach based on independent human thought. This became known as philosophy. Two questions they examined were: What is the nature of reality? How is knowledge acquired? Regarding the former, it was typically assumed that matter has always existed in some form. Theories were developed about why the world exists and appears to us in the ways we observe. But thinkers of that period had no need for an all-powerful creator to explain how everything came into being.

After 2000 BC, a belief developed in the western Mediterranean that there was one God who had revealed his will to his chosen people, the Hebrews. The idea of this God continued over into Christianity, where certain believers wrote accounts of the life and teachings of Jesus. These writings, which claimed to have been inspired by the one true God, became authoritative for the followers of Jesus and formed the basis of Church teachings.

Until the modern era, which began around the 16th century, most monotheistic traditions had some form of belief in an all-powerful being. Then followed a period in Western thought when the idea that a supreme being was necessary to explain the origins of everything we know seemed to have lost all meaning. More recently, theorists such as the philosopher Bertrand Russell and the biologist Richard Dawkins have argued that religious belief is unscientific, misguided, or even dangerous. Associated with this position is the idea that human beings, particularly those living in democratic societies, have been emancipated from the constraints of authoritarian religious dogma.

In most modern societies, truth is equated with the correctness of facts. This applies just as much to religious questions as it does to our everyday physical world experience. For example, the idea that there is one God, Allah, and Muhammad is his prophet, is as true for Muslims as the idea that the earth is round. But more recently, what was regarded as the unassailable truths of our existence have become enveloped in a fundamental ambiguity. For example, it was initially believed that light consisted of waves or particles. Then quantum theory revealed that particles also have a wave-like nature and that all matter exhibits both wave and particle properties. Since they have no definable location, the particles of which everything is made are seen as having an intrinsic connectedness. No ultimate separation can therefore exist between individual beings and objects.

Exploring God through revelation, reason and experience

By the time of the Protestant Reformation in the 16th century, Church and State had become so entwined that the persecution of non-Catholics was officially sanctioned. Many of the oppressed adopted a retaliatory approach. Later, in the post-Reformation wars between Protestant England and Catholic Spain and France, people on both sides were killed purely for their religious beliefs.

A similar situation exists today in certain Muslim countries where the death penalty is imposed on those who convert from Islam to another faith. Just as had occurred in Europe, a particular interpretation of God's revelation is regarded as the absolute truth, and no provision is made for people to hold alternative views. The rational capacities of individuals are thereby devalued with disastrous consequences for the societies involved. Although the use of reason alone cannot establish the existence of God, it is one of the factors that is generally regarded as significant in evaluating the relevant evidence.

In the Christian tradition, early theologians and philosophers argued about whether our knowledge of God comes only through divine revelation or whether human reason has a role to play. Then in the 13th century, Thomas Aquinas taught that while we can believe in the existence of God through observing the workings of nature, the attributes of God can only be revealed through scripture and the teachings of the Church.

Several centuries later, rapid developments in scientific knowledge led to increased confidence in the value of human endeavor and the exercise of reason, which certain philosophers relied on to validate religious doctrines.

The above included the 17th century philosopher Rene Descartes. He proposed that because he could not doubt his own existence, he was similarly free from doubt regarding the idea of a supremely perfect being. John Locke argued that the necessity for belief in God lies in the importance of morality, which in his view is grounded in the law of reason.

In the thought of Leibniz, the existence of a created order reflects the idea that something that actually exists has a greater degree of perfection than something that is merely possible. The resurrection of Jesus is then interpreted as a divine act that enabled a human body to achieve a more perfect form.

A different argument for the existence of God was made by Immanuel Kant. His claim was that although we can have no proof that a divine being exists, our moral sense suggests the idea that God is the originator of those feelings.

On the question of God's existence, equal weight has at times been given to conclusions based on the exercise of reason and those arising from the experience of faith. But even those who have a high regard for reason may place greater value on their religious experience than on their rational abilities. For example, Descartes claimed to have received his ideas in a vision. He described divine revelation of this kind as being more certain than knowledge acquired through reason. Similarly, the 20th-century philosopher Edmund Husserl regarded his immediate awareness of God as more fundamental than any evidence that could be advanced for his existence. For Husserl, faith that comes from the heart and will has a more profound significance than ideas originating in the mind.

A philosopher whose experience lacked the awareness of God is Friedrich Nietzsche. Having proposed that the God of traditional beliefs is "dead," Nietzsche challenged the negative view of the human being as expressed in Christianity. He claimed that this religion's obsession with questions of morality provides no outlet for bodily instincts, which are thought of in terms of evil temptations. Nietzsche's remedy was that we find a God who epitomizes the value of life itself.

Blaise Pascal rejected the idea that we can acquire knowledge through either reason or experience. He claimed that we have insufficient evidence to prove the existence or non-existence of God. Christianity teaches that those who believe in God as revealed in Jesus Christ will have happiness in this life and an infinity of happiness in the life to come. Those who do not believe will suffer eternal punishment in hell. Because of these facts, Pascal argued that the most prudent thing for a non-believer to do is weigh up the odds as to which will be the most beneficial—a life of believing in God and following his ways or one of refusing to believe. Pascal presented this choice in terms of making a wager or a bet based solely on self-interest. If God exists, Pascal claims, the benefits in this world of a relationship with him outweigh any benefits that could be claimed for a life of non-belief.

Reflections on the philosophers

As I considered the various ways philosophers have discussed the existence of God, I concluded that no one argument or type of experience can demonstrate either God's existence or what a relationship with him would be like. So I then turned to alternative accounts of attempts to reach out to the ultimate mystery. These included the story of some early believers who took a different view by claiming oneness with the divine. My interest in this particular group arose initially because of the critical comments made about their beliefs by preachers in the orthodox tradition.

The origins of Gnosticism

After Jesus died, various manuscripts appeared outlining who he was, the events of his life and teaching, and the nature of his purposes in the lives of his followers. By the end of the 2nd century, what eventually became the official Church had become a hierarchical institution of bishops, priests, and deacons. Creeds and doctrines were formulated, and no deviation from authorized teachings was permitted. By the 4th century, it had been decided which manuscripts were to be included in the official bible of the Church. During that period, Christianity was given official status by the Roman Emperor Constantine 1. It quickly became the dominant religion of the empire.

Then, in 1945, a collection of early Christian texts was discovered hidden in a stone jar concealed inside a cave near the Upper Egyptian town of Nag Hammadi, which outlined an alternative approach to sacred truth that ran concurrently with the official view.

The Nag Hammadi writings contain gospels that describe Jesus' life and at least one of the authors were among the original group of his disciples. Among them is the Gospel of Thomas, dating from the first century CE, which is one of the first of such accounts to be written. It includes material recorded in the biblical gospels, which focuses on the possibility of becoming one with the divine. Today these writers are referred to as Gnostics—a term derived from the Greek word "gnosis"—the kind of knowledge gained through direct spiritual insight.

The idea of becoming one with God I found most interesting, particularly as it seemed to reflect the prayer Jesus offered for his followers: "that they may all be one, just as you, Father, are in me, and I in you."

Regarding who Jesus was, the orthodox position identified him as God in human form. But to the Gnostics, Jesus was not God, but one who taught about the divine light within us all. He demonstrated this kind of life so that we could follow his example.

A central teaching of Gnosticism is that to know the self at the deepest level is to know God. A second-century Gnostic, Marcus, believed that everyone was part of the same whole and that this oneness will be restored when we choose to see past the illusion of separation. For the Gnostics, our true home is a realm of light—a place outside matter. They taught that we are multidimensional beings who are connected to the universe, which contains parallel dimensions beyond the three we know in our everyday lives—width, length and height. Upon our original descent into mortality, we left behind our divine image, forgetting our true origin. The task we now have is to find our way back to the realm of light to be reunited with God. Because we are of divine origin, we can pursue this goal in our earthly lives through a union with the "divine spark," or the God within us. Whereas believers within the Church had to exercise faith in a supernatural being taught by the religious authorities, Gnostics believed they had evolved beyond that level by connecting with their inner light. In the Gospel of Thomas, Jesus says that there is a light within each person, and it lights up the whole universe. Lee Hager suggests that for Gnostics, God is not an entity outside the universe, nor is God's kingdom a place or a thing, but rather a spiritual reality permeating everything in existence.

One of the teachings of Gnosticism concerned the question of creation. Like some other groups in the early Church period, Gnostics held that everything is an emanation from the one eternal source and that the human soul is spiritual and immortal. Against this view, the traditionalists argued that human beings could not be on a par with God, so the soul could not be part of God. The orthodox view, which has remained till this day, is that God created souls, physical bodies and the rest of the material universe out of nothing.

As the ultimate authorities on doctrine, the early Church fathers sought to discredit the Gnostics by portraying their ideas as absurd and misguided and casting false aspersions on their moral behavior. After some time, Gnosticism was declared a heresy. Its members were persecuted by the Church, and many were tortured and put to death. Most of their writings were destroyed. Official teaching was based on the idea that salvation belonged to the Church and its sacraments and could never depend on personal experience. When Constantine declared Christianity to be the state religion in the 4th century, the killing of Gnostics was officially sanctioned on the grounds that they were potential enemies of the social order. But the most powerful motivation for these punitive acts was the belief that through his servants God was visiting judgment upon His enemies—those who held different ideas from the doctrines proclaimed by the Church. Such individuals were later described as worse than pagans, Muslims or Jews since they were said to have betrayed Christ.

I found it difficult to believe that people who claim to have found "the truth" could willingly be involved in such evil acts. I also wondered about a possible link between the idea of oneness with the divine and the behavior of those who embraced that belief. I then began to explore the historical development of this way of engaging with ultimate reality.

Mystical experience

Mysticism grew in the medieval period, where the authoritarian structures of the Church were bypassed in favor of personal spiritual journeys. As long as individuals recognized the gulf separating them from God, no action was taken by the authorities. But anyone claiming experience of some kind of identity with the divine was at risk of excommunication or legal action. Even the great theologian and mystic Meister Eckhart was tried for heresy by Pope John XXII in the 14th century for writing statements suggesting that he and God were one being.

The practice of mysticism has been known in most cultures throughout history. But one difficulty in determining whether these practices can shed any light on the meaning of existence lies in understanding the nature of the experiences themselves. In what has been described as altered states of consciousness, the awareness of self disappears, and individual things seem to lose their independent existence as everything is absorbed into a mysterious oneness. Accessing this state requires that the mind is completely still and detached from all objects of desire. Reports of mystical experiences include a cessation of all sensory capacity and reasoning functions and a feeling of timelessness and spacelessness. Mystics describe a sense of peace and bliss in the loss of their identifiable selves and as being in a vast and profound solitude.

There have always been individuals and groups of people within the monotheisms who claim to have had mystical experiences of various kinds. Religions have then had to determine the extent to which these experiences can be incorporated into orthodox doctrines. There have been times when mystics have been regarded as possessing unique insights into truth, and the material they present has been used to reinforce the teachings of the particular tradition. On other occasions, their ideas have been seen as dangerous or subversive. Mystics themselves can be divided into two groups: those who desire to be absorbed into unity with God or the ultimate mystery, and those who believe a gulf exists between human beings and their Creator and who seek merely an intimate relationship with him.

Certain accounts given by mystics in the medieval period involve the desire to be united with Christ, and an understanding that an individual can never be identical with the divine. Catherine of Sienna was said to have undergone states of penance from a young age, praying almost continually, fasting, and sleeping little. She claims to have celebrated a mystical marriage to Christ in her twenties. A further example is Teresa of Avila, who had various experiences, including losing her personal identity, mental functioning, and sensory capacities. She ultimately attained what she believed was a spiritual union with Christ, which she describes in terms of sexual intimacy.

The experiences of medieval mystics could suggest that the divine is mysteriously accessible in these kinds of encounters. However, this does not explain the significant differences in interpreting such experiences recounted by individuals of various religious persuasions. For example, the experience of a Jewish or Muslim mystic would not involve marriage to Christ. Differences of this kind are in sharp contrast to the similarities in the states of union described by mystics from the various traditions where all identity awareness disappears. The discovery that the mind can transcend the limitations of our everyday functioning suggests that what is experienced in these altered states of consciousness indicates a different dimension of reality, which can be accessed independently of any belief system and is beyond the ability of language to describe.

The sense of oneness experienced by mystics is consistent with the discovery made by quantum theorists that, ultimately, there are no divisions within the everyday reality we encounter. This understanding made me even more interested in pursuing an alternative view of the nature of our existence. When I first heard about quantum theory, I wished that I'd had a scientific background to explore the subject further. I then found several books written by outstanding cosmologists for the general public. I spent a great deal of time working on the ideas they were presenting.

Quantum discoveries

In the early 20th century, the study of light, which was initially thought to consist of either particles or electromagnetic waves, revealed that light has both wave-like and particle-like properties. Experiments showed that a wave spreads out over an immeasurable distance when it is not observed but collapses into a particle state when it is. Because they have no actual location, the particles of which everything is made are seen as having an intrinsic connectedness, and the normal separateness we observe is merely an illusion. The concept of an indivisible universe means that no ultimate separation can exist between an observer who conducts an experiment, the apparatus used, and the findings obtained. Beyond the self-contained identities of our daily existence is a mysterious unity from which all individual phenomena arise.

One group of mathematical cosmologists suggested that the universe extends beyond the three dimensions of our daily existence. An earlier investigation of higher dimensions conducted in the 1970s proposed that the basic building blocks of the universe are strings that vibrate at different frequencies, giving rise to various forms of matter and energy. In the mid-1990s, these string theorists determined that there are ten dimensions of space and one of time.

The above approach provides an alternative to the big bang theory, based on the idea that the universe began with a random quantum fluctuation occurring at a particular point. Religious leaders have used the Big Bang Theory to support the idea that a personal God brought everything into being out of nothing. By contrast, string theory proposes the existence of an endless source of matter and energy, where the universe has the power to perpetuate itself indefinitely.

A conscious universe

A further indication of our connectedness with the universe comes from studies of the relationship between thought and matter. Some scientists hold the view that consciousness and matter are mutually exclusive concepts. Others believe that consciousness is a product of the brain. An alternative approach involves reducing everything to the physical so that all reality, including consciousness, is held to consist merely of material interactions.

Theorists who oppose these views regard consciousness as the fundamental reality. Biologists have pointed out that a primitive form of consciousness can be seen in the activity of the cell, where a DNA molecule copies itself to produce two identical molecules. The body's various organs are formed through the ongoing process of cell division. Cells somehow "know" how to differentiate and pass the required information to subsequent cells.

Quantum discoveries have led to a new understanding of the universe. As a result, many scientists now accept that the universe is conscious. The writers of religious texts obviously did not have access to such information, so believers have been reluctant to accept the idea that matter is conscious. Instead, they rely on the biblical account that God formed Adam from dust and gave him the breath of life. Consciousness or life is thereby seen as a gift bestowed on human beings, with matter itself remaining lifeless.

The religious approach

A fundamental doctrine in religious traditions is that we are separated from God because of our sinfulness and disobedience to his commands. The Hebrew scriptures depict God's view of his creatures as "disloyal and rotten to the core." This idea of universal human depravity is carried over into Christianity, where it is endorsed by St. Paul. Both Christianity and Islam describe hell as a place of eternal punishment for those who refuse to believe in God.

The idea of a fundamental separation of human beings from their creator is at odds with modern scientific discoveries about the intrinsic connectedness of everything that exists. Similarly, the doctrine of separation conflicts with the sense of oneness described by mystics in the various traditions.

This divergence of views was brought to the fore when new religions were established. While their founders and some early followers had experiences of oneness, many later followers reinterpreted these experiences so that they became a system of doctrines forming the basis for a relationship with God. Power fell into the hands of a few who claimed the right to determine "correct" teachings and to decree the eternal fate of non-believers. These leaders, who were exclusively male, have tended to assume a God-like role in dispensing judgments and punishments.

It seemed that the traditional belief of humanity's estrangement from God, together with the idea that matter is lifeless, needed to be replaced by the idea that the source of all existence is the conscious universe. The oneness described by mystics and reinforced by modern scientific theory leaves no place for a God who is totally separate from creation. It is instead the case that we each participate in the mysterious union that underlies the whole of reality.

The value of religious experience

Up to this point, religious concepts have been addressed mainly in the context of experiences recounted by mystics. While most believers do not enter into the altered states of consciousness that characterize the mystical state, some describe their experiences as life-transforming and claim that they have found meaning, purpose, and hope through their faith. The intense and intimate nature of these experiences has been claimed by believers and certain religious thinkers to demonstrate the reality of God's existence.

In studies carried out in Kuwait, college students were asked whether they had changed profoundly due to a religious experience. Forty-eight per cent of men and fifty-two percent of women said they had. Religious belief in general has been shown to alleviate the fear of death and help overcome addictions and life-negating behaviors. It can promote psychological growth and lead to feelings of safety and peace by providing comfort and hope, courage, guidance, and moral strength.

Arguments for the existence of God based on religious experience are inadequate to establish conclusively that a personal God exists. On the other hand, many people have sufficiently powerful experiences to become believers or to have their faith in God confirmed. From the evidence available, it is difficult to deny that something out of the ordinary is happening in these people's lives, both in terms of the intensity of their experiences, and the life changes that result.

Other paths to transformation

It is not only religions that claim to have answers to the human condition. Many books have been published by individuals claiming to have had life-transforming experiences in recent times. According to the authors, similar experiences are available to anyone willing to accept the ideas they outline and take the steps they prescribe. Although they may have no interest in the concept of a personal, transcendent God, these authors advocate their own particular beliefs and methods with a zeal that parallels the approach of theists who claim their deity is the one true God and that only he can meet an individual's deepest needs. Both groups seem to assume that other systems of beliefs and practices are either wrong or lacking in certain essential elements.

Apart from the writers of self-help books, alternatives theories are advanced by members of the helping professions concerned with the problems of everyday living. In these disciplines, it is commonly believed that we all can meet our need for wholeness or integration. Attention is often given to those deep areas of consciousness that are not immediately accessible to the person but are believed to influence feelings and behavior. Most forms of therapy hold that what we think at a conscious level may have little relationship to our beliefs at a much deeper level. For example, a woman who is outstandingly successful in her career and as a wife and mother, may have endured overwhelming pain in her formative years. Although she may consciously believe that she is a worthwhile person, she may see herself as worthless at a much deeper level of consciousness. In the safety of the therapeutic setting, memories of earlier painful experiences can be uncovered and if she comes to recognize her intrinsic worth through this process, her life may be transformed.

Just as the various religious traditions each claim to have access to the truth, opinions vary in the helping professions as to which approach will be the most effective way of providing help for a client. Among the earlier psychological theorists, conflicting views were advanced regarding the effects of sexual repression, the need to integrate the diverse elements of the psyche or the striving for power. Later approaches addressed the impact of conditioning and the unrecognized beliefs that control our behavior. A similar situation exists in the self-help movement, where authors discuss their own unique methods of finding peace after periods of despair.

Because of the wide variations among systems of thought that offer the hope of personal transformation, it seemed evident that no single set of ideas could have a valid claim to be effective for everyone. My theory is that whether a particular set of beliefs has the potential to be life-transforming for a given person usually depends on the degree of compatibility between the ideas themselves and the personality structure of the individual, together with the cumulative effects of changing circumstances and influences in the person's life. William James suggests that religion is only one of many ways of remedying inner incompleteness. His view is that this is a general psychological process that can have an intellectual basis.

Gillian Ross describes the yearning to connect with something that seems to be beyond or greater than ourselves as our primary aspiration. Similarly, Václav Havel writes of the need for transcendence—a state he describes as being in harmony with what seems distant from us in time and space but with which we are mysteriously linked.

The multidimensionality of existence

I was fascinated when I first heard the view proposed by string theorists that the universe is in ten spatial dimensions, and that we as humans are multidimensional beings. This claim, it seemed to me, has direct relevance to the question of beliefs and personal transformation. If our entire existence, including our consciousness, were nothing more than three-dimensional materiality, it would seem unlikely that we could experience a sense of connectedness to something greater than ourselves or even have a longing for that ultimate state of being.

When I read that the experience of union can be obtained through altered states of consciousness, it became clear to me that the paths leading to these mystical states will vary according to the life circumstances and capacities of the individual. I was interested in theorists' views in various fields, particularly those who have claimed that our minds are individual expressions of the universal mind. Karen Armstrong, the New York Times bestselling author of *The History of God*, replaces the traditional view of God as a separate, external reality with the idea that the divine is one with the ground of each person's being. Similarly, within Sufism, the universe is seen as a global being whose faculties find expression in human beings and every other aspect of reality. Ibn Arabi writes that the universe discovers itself through our discovery that it is one with us.

The above ideas reflect the views of the psychiatrist and developer of transpersonal psychology, Stanislav Grof, who writes that we can reach an experiential identification with what he calls Absolute Consciousness. In doing this, we realize that our own being is commensurate with all of existence so that we possess a divine nature.

The ultimate conclusion

My journey through philosophy was confusing because of the wide variety of experiences they described and their differing arguments about the existence of God. Similarly, the alternative approaches provided no clear path to understanding the purpose of our existence. But the link between quantum theory and mystical experience caused me to appreciate the oneness of all reality and to realize that we are each an integral part of that ultimate mystery.

Our desire to know who we are and what we can become can be understood by how a particular set of ideas translates within our individual personality structure. In this situation, the rightness or wrongness of a set of beliefs becomes irrelevant. It may happen that a person raised in a strongly religious family or culture will initially accept the beliefs of that faith. But should those ideas not resonate deeply at the experiential level, she may decide to have nothing to do with religion. Alternatively, she may adopt a similar approach to my own and decide to investigate other ways of thinking.

Many people raised in nominally Christian cultures have converted to Islam in recent years. It is estimated that in the United States, up to 25,000 people per year become Muslims. In research conducted on the reasons for these changes, the primary reported factors were the appeal of Muslim moral values and dissatisfaction with the previously accepted faith. Cases have similarly been recorded where people from an Islamic tradition have converted to Christianity or Judaism.

Those who believe the tenets of their faith to be both accurate and binding on all humanity may overlook the fact that transformation is not just a question of commitment. While some changes in behavior may occur at an outward level, genuine transformation occurs from within—at a level to which the person may not have direct access. Members of deeply religious cultures who are little affected by such beliefs may simply conform to the various requirements without considering the more profound implications of their beliefs. On the other hand, my experience showed that a devout person who believes what she has been taught about the one true God may feel like a failure when she sees evidence of transformation in others but none in herself. I formed the view that a different set of ideas might have the desired effect in cases such as this. These could include the concepts underlying an alternative faith tradition, a particular form of therapy, or the work of a self-help writer. The fact that we can experience life transformation through engaging with any of these systems of thought demonstrates that none of them can claim universal validity.

Accounts given by mystics involve contact with a dimension beyond language's ability to describe. Some theorists interpret such phenomena as representing contact with the divine, thereby confirming his existence. The idea that the reality accessed by mystics is a feature of the universe itself rather than pointing to the existence of a personal God attracted me. This, however, caused me to wonder whether a person who regards the universe as the ultimate reality could receive all the benefits claimed to occur in the lives of traditional believers.

What also concerned me was why some people experience a sense of connection to that oneness by believing something that might be factually inaccurate, while other equally ardent believers do not. And I wondered why people who have no interest in these questions could experience that kind of life transformation. The conclusion I reached was that although people holding these differing perspectives may lack a conscious awareness of this ultimate dimension, at some deep level they may be drawn toward it.

My belief is that transformation occurs when we accept the oneness of all reality and open our innermost being to the possibility of experiencing that oneness.

References

Ad-Dab'bagh, Yasser. "The Transformative Effect of Seeking the Eternal: A Sampling of the Perspectives of Two Great Muslim Intellectuals— Ibn-Hazm and Al-Ghazali." *Psychoanalytic Inquiry,* 28, 5, 2008.

Al'Arabi, Ibn. *Ringstones of Wisdom*. Translated by Caner K. Dagli. Berlin: momoxGmbH, 2004.

Armstrong, Karen. *Islam: A Short History*. New York: The Modern Library, 2002.

Aristotle *Physics: Book VIII*. Translated by Daniel W. Graham. Oxford: Oxford University Press, 1999.

Ash, David. *Vortex of Energy: A Scientific Theory*. Berkshire, UK: Puja Power Publications, 2012.

Birch, Charles. *On Purpose*. Sydney: New South Wales University Press, 1990.

Bohm, David. *Wholeness and the Implicate Order*. London: Routledge & Kegan Paul, 1980.

Bowlby, John. *Attachment and Loss*, Vol. 1, Attachment. New York: Basic Books, 1982.

Chara, Paul and Jill N. Gillett. "Sensory Images of God: Divine Synesthesia?" *Journal of Psychology and Christianity*, 23, 3, 2004.

Clark, J.M. *Meister Eckhart*. London: Nelson & Sons, 1957.

Cook, Daniel J. "Leibniz on 'prophets', prophecy, and revelation," *Religious Studies*, 45, 2009.

Corliss, William R. "Quantum mechanics is definitely spooky." *Science Frontiers,* No. 114, Nov-Dec 1997.

Davies, Paul. *God and the New Physics.* London: Penguin Books Ltd., 1983.

Derrida, Jacques. *On the Name.* Edited and translated by Thomas Dutoit. Stanford: Stanford University Press, 1995.

Descartes, René. *Principles of Philosophy,* Translated by John Veitch. Montana: Kessinger Publishing. 2004.

Dyson, Freeman. *Infinite in All Directions.* New York: Harper & Row, 1988.

Ewing, Alfred C. "Awareness of God." *Philosophy,* 40, no. 151, 1965.

Franks Davis, Caroline. *The Evidential Force of Religious Experience.* Oxford: Clarendon Press, 1989.

Gonzáles, Alessandra L. "Measuring Religiosity in a Majority Muslim Context: Gender, Religious Salience and Religious Experience Among Kuwaiti College Students—A Research Note," *Journal for the Scientific Study of Religion,* 50, 2, 2011.

Greene, Brian. *The Elegant Universe: Superstrings, Hidden Dimensions, and the Quest for the Ultimate Theory,* W.W. Norton, 1999.

Grof, Stanislav. *The Cosmic Game: Explorations in the Frontiers of Human Consciousness.* New York: State University of New York Press, 1998.

Hadi, Fawzyiah and Ghenaim Al-Fayez. "Islamic Arabic Youth and Family Development." *Handbook of Applied Developmental Science, 3.* Edited by Richard M. Lerner. Thousand Oaks, CA: Sage Publications Inc., 2003.

Havel, Václav. "A sense of the transcendent," in *The Art of the Impossible: Politics as Morality in Practice.* New York: Knopf, 1997.

James, William. *Essays in Radical Empiricism.* New York: Cosimo Inc., 2008.

James, William. *The Varieties of Religious Experience: A Study in Human Nature.* New York: Longmans, Green, and Co., 1902.

Kant, Immanuel. *The Critique of Practical Reason.* Translated by Thomas Kingsmill Abbott. New York: Barnes & Noble Publishing, 2004.

Kirkpatrick, Lee A. and Phillip R. Shaver. "Attachment Theory and Religion: Childhood Attachments, Religious Experience, and Conversion." *Journal for the Scientific Study of Religion,* 29, 3, 1990.

Kumari, Anupam and R. S. Pirta. "Exploring Human Relationship with God as a Secure Base." *Journal of the Indian Academy of Applied Psychology,* 35, October 2009.

Locke, John. "The Reasonableness of Christianity." *The Works of John Locke* Vol. VII. London: Otridge & Son et al., 1812.

McGinn, Colin. *The Problem of Consciousness: Essays Toward a Resolution.* Malden, MA: Blackwell, 1991.

McTaggart, Lynne. *The Field: The Quest for the Secret Force of the Universe.* London: HarperCollins, 2009.

Neaman, Judith S. "Potentiation, Elevation, Acceleration: Prerogatives of Women Mystics," *Mystics Quarterly,* 14, 1, 1988.

Nietzsche, Friedrich. "Morality as Anti-Nature." *Twilight of the Idols.* New York: Oxford University Press, 1998.

Pagels, Elaine. *Beyond Belief: The Secret Gospel of Thomas.* New York: Random House, 2003.

Pascal, Blaise. *Pensées.* Translated by A.J. Krailsheimer. London: Penguin Books, 1966.

Pylkkänen, Paavo. *Mind, Matter, and the Implicate Order.* New York: Springer, 2007.

Ross, Gillian. *Psyche's Yearning: Radical Perspectives on Self Transformation.* Bloomington, IN: Trafford Publishing, 2010.

Schorsch, Ismar. "The Sacred Cluster: The Core Values of Conservative Judaism," 1995. *https://www.jewishvirtuallibrary.org/the-core-values-of-conservative-judaism*

Schwartz, Arthur J. "The Nature of Spiritual Transformation: A Review of the Literature," 2000.

Śesharāva More, *Islam, maker of the Muslim mind*, Pune, India: Rajhans Prakashan, 2004.

Stapp, Henry P. "Why Classical Mechanics Cannot Naturally Accommodate Consciousness But Quantum Mechanics Can," 2008.

Strawson, Galen. "Realistic monism: why physicalism entails panpsychism." *Journal of Consciousness Studies*, 13, 2006.

Thomas Aquinas, Summa Theologica: Vol. 1 of 10. Translated by Dominican Province. Charleston SC, USA: Forgotten Books, 2007.

Zangwill, Nick. "The myth of religious experience." *Religious Studies*, 40, 2004.

Zinnbauer, Brian J. and Kenneth I. Pargament. "Spiritual Conversion: A Study of Religious Change Among College Students." *Journal for the Scientific Study of Religion*, 37, 1, 1998.

About the Author

Lynne Renoir was born in Brisbane, Australia in 1941. She was the eldest daughter of an evangelist who believed every word in the Bible had been dictated by God. This led him to the view that his child had been born in sin, and that it was his duty to belt the devil out of her. The frequent physical punishments Lynne received caused her not only psychological damage but a feeling that she had somehow failed God. This situation led her on a long quest to discover whether she was, in fact, a failure, or whether her father had been mistaken in his beliefs.

In pursuing this question, Lynne completed a Master's degree in Psychology, followed by a PhD in Philosophy. She formed the view that her father's behavior was the result of serious deficiencies in his upbringing, together with his absorption of a distorted interpretation of the biblical text.

Lynne was motivated to share her findings in two books, *God Interrogated: Reinterpreting the Divine*, and *Leaving Faith, Finding Meaning: A Preacher's Daughter's Search for God*. In these works Lynne analyzes the various ways thinkers have researched questions of ultimate reality. She concludes that there is no one correct answer in this complex area of thought, and that different approaches may lead to the kind of transformation that is sought by those who long for meaning in their lives.

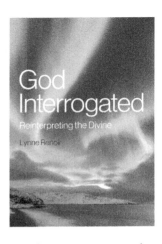

God Interrogated –
Reinterpreting the Divine

In this work, Lynne Renoir questions the traditional view of God as an all-powerful being who created the universe and governs it according to his will. She argues that such an idea can be challenged philosophically, and that it does not accord with discoveries in modern science. On the other hand, she suggests, it is evident that experiences of transformation can occur in the lives of individuals who wholeheartedly embrace religious beliefs.

God Interrogated explores possible explanations for this situation by proposing that truth is found in the inner dimensions of a person's being, and is not something that can be imposed from an external source.

Lynne Renoir's work was the result of her own difficulties in experiencing the transformation she sought through her Christian faith, and followed years of research undertaken in the areas of philosophy, psychology, and quantum science.

God Interrogated - Reinterpreting the Divine

is published by John Hunt and will be available in Spring 2023.

Read Lynne Renoir's blog posts and download excerpts from her books at

www.lynnerenoir.com

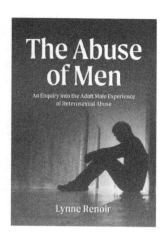

The Abuse of Men
An Enquiry into the Adult Male Experience
of Heterosexual Abuse

Lynne Renoir, suffered physical abuse at the hands of her judgmental father. The pain she endured led her to investigate how other abused people suffer, particularly men in their relationships with destructive women.

In her Master's thesis Lynne interviewed forty-eight men from Australia and New Zealand. They told her about severe physical, psychological and sexual abuse. This led her to the view that men, as a whole, have been disempowered.

She points to the fact that society sees only women as victims of abuse, with men inevitably portrayed as perpetrators. Her call is for governmental authorities to recognize the plight of men in abusive relationships and to take action to remedy the wrong that has been done to them.

The Abuse of Men

is available in digital format for all E-readers including Kindle

Read Lynne Renoir's blog posts and download excerpts from her books at

www.lynnerenoir.com

Made in United States
North Haven, CT
08 May 2023

36373727R00134